*Un*conventions

WRITINGS ON WRITING BY Michael Martone

Unconventions

Attempting the Art of Craft and the Craft of Art

The University of Georgia Press   Athens and London

Published by The University of Georgia Press
Athens, Georgia 30602
© 2005 by Michael Martone

Designed by Sandra Strother Hudson
Set in Berkeley Oldstyle Medium
Printed and bound by Maple-Vail
The paper in this book meets the guidelines for permanence
and durability of the Committee on Production Guidelines
for Book Longevity of the Council on Library Resources.
Printed in the United States of America
09 08 07 06 05 C 5 4 3 2 1
09 08 07 06 05 P 5 4 3 2 1

Library of Congress Cataloging-in-Publication Data
Martone, Michael.
Unconventions : attempting the art of craft and the craft
of art : writings on writing / by Michael Martone.
        p.   cm.
Includes bibliographical references.
ISBN-13: 978-0-8203-2778-5 (alk. paper)
ISBN-10: 0-8203-2778-6 (alk. paper)
ISBN-13: 978-0-8203-2779-2 (pbk. : alk. paper)
ISBN-10: 0-8203-2779-4 (pbk. : alk. paper)
1. Martone, Michael—Authorship. 2. Authorship. I. Title.
PS3563.A7414U53 2005
808'.02—dc22   2005017321

British Library Cataloging-in-Publication Data available

For my students now teaching

Contents

Acknowledgments

I wish to thank Peter Turchi and the faculty at the MFA Program for Writers at Warren Wilson College, where many of these pieces were first delivered, and the AWP and its director, David Fenza, who also provided a convention platform and parliament of press for these papers. R.,M. Berry, W. Scott Olsen, John Witte, David Milofsky, Vincent Standley, Paul Maliszewski, and the editors of *Southern Indiana Review, Symplokē, Mississippi Review, Sycamore Review, Ascent, American Literary Review,* and the *Electronic Book Review* for fixing them in print. I acknowledge my home delegation: Susan Neville, Nancy Esposito, Valerie Miner, Michael Rosen, Valerie Berry, Sandy Huss, Robin Behn, Wendy Rawlings, Joel Brouwer, Joyelle McSweeney, Patti White, John Crowley, Melanie Rae Thon, Monroe Engel, Susan Dodd, Chris Leland, Lewis Hyde, Joe Geha, Steve Pett, Scott Sanders, and Jay Brandon. Here's to the founding committee of RKO Radio Poems—Jan, Geoff, and Mike. Thank you Nicole Mitchell, Mindy Wilson, and dignitaries at the University of Georgia Press, and Marian Young, who wrote the enabling language. Kathy Hall always contradicted and was always right. And, as before, I second Theresa Pappas, the unacknowledged legislator acknowledged here.

# Love a Parade

AN AFTERWORD

The unit in front of me is a freshly detailed Ford Mustang convertible transporting (the hand-painted sign reads) Little Miss Cutie Pie of Western Alabama. Behind me is another gleaming convertible, a pastel Caddy this time, where, in its backseat, the reigning Miss Junior Petite Darling of Tuscaloosa County purposely practices her waving. I constitute a unit of one, on foot, standing in the middle of the street between the idling cars packed with beauty contest princesses, cooling my heels in the staging area, waiting for the annual Labor Day parade to begin.

Some explanation is in order. Yes there is, even in Alabama, a presence of organized labor, one strong enough to mount an annual parade each fall. The Labor Council is composed of various locals—mineworkers, autoworkers, state employees, teachers, and all the crafts and all the trades of construction— electrical, plumbing, painting. The locals all provide their own floats or decked-out trucks, supported by a phalanx of members on foot, toting picket signs, banners, and flags. The council invites entrants from the community to join the procession. There are high school marching bands, church vans, dance schools, radio station SUVs, mounted sheriffs' posses, motorcycle clubs, and the seemingly endless convoy of princesses and beauty queens, some of them representing the local products and produce—cotton, peanuts, hogs, and mules. Then there is me. I am wearing a pink shirt, a faded indication of solidarity, I tell myself. But I am otherwise anonymous—no placard, no preceding majorette team with signage, not even a sandwich board to let the crowd know who I am, what I represent. I walk down the center of the street, following the dashes of the yellow traffic stripe. The route is two miles long and will end up in a park past the courthouse where a picnic will commence. The governor, Fob James, will be there, pressing the flesh, and I will get to shake his hand.

But this still does not explain what I am doing, in my pink shirt, marching in the Labor Day parade. I am a writer after all. My trade and craft is literary fiction and nonfiction. I don't work on the line but work a line, convey stories, produce prose. It is a solitary task, writing, not one usually lent to collective bargaining or so I imagine most people imagine. But still, I am in good standing, a card-carrying, dues-paying member of the entity known as the National Writers Union.

I have always liked the cognitive dissonance such an organization and membership in it creates—the category of writer so easily maintained as separate from the category of trade unionist. My membership makes me, and people who know me as a writer, ask existential questions. Just what is a writer? What's the writer's job? Is writing craft, art, hobby, or mere busy-work? But wait, it gets better.

I belong to the New York City local even though I live in Alabama—no local in Tuscaloosa, no other members in Alabama as far as I know. A few years ago the National Writers Union, living close to the bone as you might guess, affiliated with the UAW, the United Auto Workers, the famous and storied industrial organization of Detroit, Michigan, and its deep pockets. So I am, officially, an autoworker. I belong to an association of autoworkers and reap the benefits of the representation. I have a union credit card. I get a discount renting a car. The National Writers Union is local 1981 in the UAW's lineup. I receive the magazine, *Solidarity*, where they feature, from time to time, the goings-on of the writers' local, buried in the pages of news reporting the Caterpillar strike or the closing of the light-truck plant at Sparrows Point. What are those writers up to?

I like the juxtaposition this creates. I like to flash my union card at my students, who are trying to figure out what it means to be a writer in America and watch them puzzle over the picture, white-, blue-, or pink-collar indeed. And I do like to elaborate the metaphor. It helps to make the abstracts I constantly construct more concrete—to think that as I write I am actually building something, making something from scratch, shaping sense like my brothers and sisters in the movement shape sheet metal.

Of course the confusion cuts both ways. When I called the Tuscaloosa Labor Council to enter the parade, I identified myself as a member of the union. Would it be possible, I asked, to march with the local locals? There's a tire factory in town, an auto parts maker, a mill. Times are tense. Organized labor in this town has been eyeing the new Mercedes plant that makes the M-Class SUV with nonunion workers. That organization effort has been slow going. I was regarded with suspicion, my request questioned. "What is it you are again?" I was asked.

And so I ended up as my own unit, sandwiched between the pageant winners who glided along via their be-chromed vehicular cloud, their union-made rides. I am sure to the lawn-chaired masses watching from the curb, I looked very curious indeed. Who is that strange pink-shirted man stalking among the princesses? I waved like a fool. The judges at the reviewing stand, I actually could see, scratched their heads, checked their clipboards. There must be some explanation. I continued to wave—word worker that I am—working the crowd, the ground shifting beneath my marching feet.

I found myself in the middle of another kind of parade, part of the surging movement and yet in its midst apart. Let's call it the march of time and taste, the parade of history.

I graduated from the Writing Seminars at Johns Hopkins in 1979, a member of the first generation of American literary writers to be completely naturalized into the curious notion (inaugurated by the cadre of WWII-benefited GIs who originated the idea) that the job of writer could be professionalized with a stint in a university workshop. The movement of writers into the university, most often as students and teachers attached to English departments, was always fraught with anxiety and continues to be. First, how would PhDed critics in an English department accommodate the new practicing instead of preaching, terminal-degreeless colleagues? Over time, however, the writers were absorbed and began minting writers, now with their own MFA degrees, who then sought teaching positions, expanding into new universities and other English departments, competing, finally, with their literature colleagues for students and positions. As the New Criticism waned to be replaced by critical theories less interested in the aesthetic appreciation of poetry and fiction and its historical assessment, writers in the university felt compelled to tend and nurture the canon, teaching more and more the models of the past, sometimes becoming, in the vacuum, more literature professor than the literature professors.

In the middle of this streaming history, I went off to school as a prose writer and wrote in workshops conducted by John Barth, Edmund White, and Charles Newman. At the end of the seventies something was up aesthetically, you might even say theoretically, in the ensconced and increasingly insulated track of creative writing.

I found myself, as a student, at the tail end of the most recent flowering of prose writing interested in formal innovation and self-conscious, metafictional styles often characterized by both its practitioners and critics as "experimental." John Barth, my teacher, had recently published celebrated books that contained stories printed on Möbius strips and narrated by sperm. His stories telescoped stories within stories to the seventh degree and were written, as the subtitle read, for voice and tape as well as the printed page. Such experiments were pervasive. Donald Barthelme, Robert Coover, Ishmael Reed, Grace Paley, Alain Robbe-Grillet, and Italo Calvino concentrated on the collage and fairy tale, and the whole scaffolding revealed the artifice of art. Anthologies of that time were titled *Innovative Fiction*, *Anti-Story*, and *Superfiction*. Realistic narratives, when they were read or written, were relegated to a diminished category, dismissed as mere secular news reports. At the moment, the way to the heart was through the brain not the gut.

But that all changed the year I graduated from Hopkins. John Gardner, the author of *Grendel*, recanting the testimony of his earlier books, published *On Moral Fiction* lamenting the prose experiments of his generation, suggesting they were products of wasted lives and talent. A new translation of Chekhov appeared. *Matters of Life and Death*, an anthology of what would be called "minimal" fiction (in contrast to the maximal work it was replacing), attacked, in its premise, the frivolity of the American short fiction published in the sixties and seventies. And Raymond Carver's book of stories *What We Talk About When We Talk About Love* arrived and changed everything. At the same time, John Barth's formally ambitious seventh novel was published. *LETTERS* is an epistolary novel that sequels, simultaneously, the author's previous six books, characters from each writing each other and to a character named the Author. The *New York Times* marked the appearance as the end of modernism and in doing so implied that we all were entering, in our little corner of the world, a brave new one, characterized by the return to realist narratives and just plain old-fashioned storytelling. The way to the heart, the new anatomy read, was through the gut.

The transformation of the literary landscape was so profound and sudden that when I visited Baltimore again in 1983, Barth mentioned wistfully that times were tough, that the competition for students was more severe. Where are they going? To Syracuse, he replied, to study with Carver, who had announced, famously, that writers learning to write should adhere to the advice of "no tricks." And that aesthetic held. For the next twenty years in the realm of short fiction produced in burgeoning creative writing programs and published in literary magazines, the realistic narrative was the dominant ideology.

I didn't know it back then, but through the accidents of time and space I came of age as a writer on the cusp of this particular paradigm shift, truly in the middle of things. Even more curious was that, six years after my sober discussion with Barth in Baltimore, I would be heading to Syracuse to teach, occupying the line Raymond Carver had vacated a few years before.

In my own work, I suppose, I have been trying to negotiate these two competing ways of making prose fiction. My stories always seem to be a little bit about, well, stories. But I also like to think they are self-conscious in a rather unconscious way. And I am certainly up to employing the tricks—authentic and nonsentimental voice, concrete detail, telling gesture, earned epiphany—promoted by the "no tricks" program. That is to say, my thesis has always been to synthesize, to understand and use any technique, any formula, any style available. I find myself, then, self-identifying as a formalist, both an experimenter and a traditionalist and yet, at the same time, neither.

I have been strangely detached, a stranger in a strange land, while watching these two extreme visions vie. I even grow wary of this analysis. Literary fiction might not be so divided and so dramatically opposed as I suggest here. I am smitten by my own illusion, my own life's story. Styles of storytelling at odds with one another make for a better story. In reality, this nasty dance of opposites repelling from each other might be just two currents in the same stream, two branches of the same tree, etc. It's a parade with both Shriners puttering past on minibikes and elephants balancing on beach balls.

I am just on my way to Swannanoa, North Carolina, to once again teach during the ten-day residence of the low-residency MFA program at Warren Wilson College. I have been making this trek since 1987, and many of the lectures and articles reprinted in this collection were originally conceived and often presented there within the intensive mix of lectures and workshops packed into the brief period the program convenes each year in the foothills of the Smoky Mountains. Because the actual time one spends with one's students and colleagues is so limited (the rest of the semester's instruction takes place virtually via electronic or postal correspondence), aesthetic issues, craft consideration, and analytic readings are delivered in concentrated and highly potent proportions with much energy, efficiency, and clarity. Students and teachers, under such time and space constraints, are forced to articulate their emerging principles of composition, their evolving taste in poetry and prose, their shifting sense of the writer's job description. I have found the setting exciting. The teaching situation there demands I regularly demolish and reconstruct my basic assumptions about my art and craft and actually perform such introspection in public (by means of lectures, talks, team-taught workshops, classes) while at the same time I witness similar public contortions and morphings being performed by the host of writers and poets present.

I think of this kind of writing as attempts. I think it is all in the attempting. After all, after all the words about words, we may, in fact, know very little about what it is we do do with words. But it is valiant, this public struggle. That is to say, the essays the reader finds here were never written with any effort to be the final word on words. They are not the authority of authorship. Secrets are not, are never, revealed and probably don't even exist in the first place. I think of these outbursts as just that, outbursts. They are in the genre of surprise, the art of the overheard, the literature of curiosity. The welling up under pressure. The forcing of narcissus in the winter.

A practicing poet, prolific and successful—whom I'll not name here—and I were in several undergraduate workshops together years ago at Indiana University. I thoroughly and constantly disagreed with him over every possible topic on the subject of writing. Casually to my classes over the years, I have confessed that I fault (or blame or praise) the poet of our shared youthful but impassioned quibbles in poetry for creating the me who is the I writing today. We would, for instance, argue constantly, endlessly on the nature and quality of our line breaks until, at the end of my rope, I went home and wrote a poem that used the "ding" of the typewriter bell to signal, midsentence, even midword, when to end the line. I think of this as my origin tale, the moment I became a prose writer, as I returned to the workshop to defend the mechanical intervention in my scansion. But it was in that very heated but, I think, very lucky confrontation that I was able (as with the pressure pedagogy practiced at Warren Wilson) to figure out many things and to find ways to keep writing. I had something to push against. The strategy of opposition, of argument, of the contrarian has stuck with me, my way of making sense or, maybe even more accurately, my way of simply sensing the boundaries, the scope, and the stakes of these arbitrary issues. This acquired habit allowed me to resist habit, to turn against any well-tuned position. A convention, then, to be unconventional. Oh, but what did I know? I was a kid and full of it. I was learning to like to hear myself talk. I liked to hear myself talk. But still, if you are out there, thanks for pushing back, opposing vector of the physics in which we still find ourselves enmeshed.

There is one last thing to mention. A book such as this one is a Frankensteinian monster, a literary invention really of this particular time and this place, a creature of the forces in play when creative writing and the teaching of creative writing moved into the academy. This is a collection of occasional pieces, writing about writing, expressed in a variety of bizarre hybrid forms — the interview, the introduction, the article, the convention address, the eulogy, the review, the afterword. We'd like to think that the main business of this business is the production of poetry, the manufactory of fiction, but what has developed over the last half century in creative writing is this kind of enabling apparatus — the nuts and bolts and Allen wrenches, the owners' manuals, the instructions in a bad translation, the 800-number customer service troubleshooting hot lines. These kinds of books, books like this one, collecting the auxiliary, the ancillary of the act of writing, are spawn of the mainline enterprise. This is writing that has become a cottage industry inside a cottage industry. My instinct is to first just acknowledge how strange a book like *Unconventions* is. The phenomenon of the writerly miscellany provides a habitat for these knockoff flocks of satellite prose orbiting the home world, making measurements and observations, doing science, spying, sending news of the weather, setting up networks, mapping, establishing weapons platforms, bouncing signals around, drifting along as junk. How busy they are and how the gravity of the planet defines and deflects the motions of these vehicles through space and time. Our clouded afterthoughts. Our atmosphere of metaphor. But maybe, and this is the contrarian speaking, just maybe, this fleet of jerry-rigged occasions might be thought of as elevated heavenly bodies, moons maybe, another kind of creative writing, creating for themselves and with their own measured cadences their own standards of elegance and beauty, as engaging (and sometimes even more engaging) as the dense solid spheres they circle. Meteors. Comets. Stardust. Those rings of Saturn, that parade of rubble, more Saturn than Saturn.

e Seated

ATTEMPTING THE ART OF CRAFT AND THE CRAFT OF ART

Pete Turchi, the director of the Warren Wilson College MFA program, proposed a panel on the subject of the craft lecture for the 2003 AWP conference in Baltimore. These remarks were later published in the magazine *3rd Bed,* number 8, edited by Vince Standley.

For a while there, I lived in Syracuse, New York, in the Westcott neighborhood not far from the university and a few blocks from the house that had been built and then inhabited by the designer and philosopher of the Arts and Crafts movement, Gustav Stickley. The distinctive furniture Stickley designed over a century ago is still produced in the same manner in factories around Syracuse. You perhaps know it as Mission Oak ("Mission" for the founder's belief in the mission of his designs as well as the influence of hand-hewn, honest pieces found in Spanish missions). It is sturdy quartersawn oak, richly stained to bring out the grain of the wood. The fine mechanism of its joinery often is exposed and incorporated into the concept of its design, upholstered in high grades of leather or with fabrics that look salvaged from medieval tapestries.

You should have seen the house. It had been divided up into several apartments. A colleague of mine, Safiya Henderson-Holmes, lived on the ground floor. Wood everywhere — built-in bookcases, carved inglenooks, cabinets with hand-cast pulls, window seats, plate rails, soffits, exposed beams, coffered ceilings, parquet floors, inlaid paneling, crown moldings—and wainscoting cut from one endless slab of slate. The fireplace was framed with metallic Roycroft tiles. The lamps and sconces were all burnished patinaed hammered copper, their leaded frames glassed with mica.

My house on Fellows Ave., a 1910 foursquare, had a few of these fixtures, oak-y trim and rustic hutch, enough to make the rocking chair and library desk scrounged in Iowa look good. Before Syracuse, I had lived in Iowa, where Mission furniture with its mission of honest craftsmanship had taken root. Before Barbra Streisand began collecting the style, bidding $350,000 for Stickley's own sideboard taken from the Syracuse house, you could get the stuff at auction or in flea markets for a song. After Streisand came Redford's *A River Runs Through It* set decorated wall to paneled wall with it, and the furniture new or used was out of sight. In fact this recent speculation sparked the factories in upstate New York to return to the designs from a century before. They had been staying in business on the strength of Chippendale knockoffs and Queen Anne copies.

Why do I bring this up, waxing nostalgic while waxing this furniture, in a lecture on the craft lecture? Analogies of course. Metaphor. I thought by evoking Stickley, the movement he engendered, the furniture itself, we might have an exemplum, a model, to consider the metaphor of craft and how this very solid idea gets applied to the more abstract carpentry of writing. I also worked very hard at that opening, demonstrating, I hope, some aspects of craft in action in writing—openings, scene setting, description, litany, consonance. My own puttering around in the workshop, whittling away at words.

I live in Tuscaloosa now, the New South, far away from the Arts and Crafts movement both temporally and geographically, in a fifties rancher that, truth be told, is not that much different from a double-wide mobile home on a concrete slab. But because this is the South, my ranch has been disguised as an antebellum mansion—brick facade, Greek pillars, wrought iron filigree—the repository for all the Chippendale knockoffs and Queen Anne copies. The Mission pieces are out of place, too massive, too solid, not a bungalow in sight. Instead I've taken to collecting at flea markets and auctions midcentury furniture of blond wood, plastic, foam, wire, chrome, vinyl, of—my god!—Naugahyde, laminates of Formica, plywood, melamine, rubber, fiberglass, canvas, aluminum, steel. Fortunately this kind of furnishing, while contemporaneous to and designed for my present kind of house, never caught on here. So the few castoffs one finds are still cheap. Fortunate too since pieces designed by Eames, Nelson, Dreyfus, Jacobsen, Saarinen, and van der Rohe are now inflating elsewhere at Streisandian velocity. You picture this stuff, right? Shell, butterfly, inflatable chairs, loungers made of cardboard, and everything, everything on wheels.

I bring up this other style of furniture for the contrast of course, not just to contrast the style of furnishings but to suggest an opposition as well in two kinds of fiction produced in workshops, reduced here to this admittedly arbitrary and artificial binary. Perhaps we can think of this with further metaphors. And writers can think of themselves in metaphorical terms.

What metaphor are you? Do you think of yourself as a craftsman or -woman, or do you think of yourself as an artist? Creative writing itself is poised as a discipline between these two metaphors, located between journalism on the one hand with its insistence upon craft and the eponymous arts department on the other with its attention on the conceptual. The inhabitants of these extremes, craft and art, view with suspicion the incursion of one realm into that of the other. Where is the art in the inverted pyramid? Where is the craft in a drip painting?

Take a look at these two chairs. Here is the Morris chair, designed by Stickley, with its wide, comfortable armrests, the mortise and tenon joinery, the chiseled railings of the side and back, the polished wood and leather pegs of the reclining mechanism. The chair says one thing clearly: I am a chair. And it reeks of craft and the craft it took to build it. Now look at Charles and Ray Eames's Shell chair, the organic sculpted fiberglass shell, the impossibly delicate lacy wire legs—it has an Eiffel base. It is bright orange, the color of a life raft. It does not say it is crafted. In fact it doesn't even look like it was man-made. In fact it wasn't man-made but made by machines. The only hand tool employed in its construction was a screwdriver anybody can handle. Here is a chair privileging home assembly with an Allen wrench above the practiced skill of the dovetail saw and handheld planer. The Eames chair says clearly: I am a sculpture. Says: What is a chair? The chairness of the first chair is settled. You sit in it. It provides comfort. The chairness of the second is up for discussion. It is far more pleasurable to look at, maybe, than to sit in. Could you fall asleep in it? Read while sitting there? You might slip out of it. You might be surprised by it. It intends to surprise you.

How one makes fiction also depends on where one is seated. Here is one kind of fiction that believes its main innovative function resides in its content. The vessel of that content, its delivery device, however, is the constant. The human in the chair is the thing in motion. The metaphorical chair of this kind of fiction has attained the ideal architecture of support. From story to story the chair must be rebuilt along the lines of its initial perfection. The other kind of fiction seeks new forms, sees the structure of the chair, of *fiction* itself as the thing in flux while the content's staying is stable. The sitting human in the chair is the constant. The possibilities of the chair, its chairness, are what are at play.

Despite its seeming definition, the craft lecture can be a useful form for the craftless story. In fact many craft lectures I have heard dwell more on theoretical, aesthetic, and conceptual issues than on technical or tactical considerations. Craft does imply that it is not the story's place to think about itself or the author's place to existentially consider authority. Craft implies an acceptance of the conventions of constructing a difficult intricate form that must be rebuilt in nearly the same way each time. Here, Craft says, are the methods and the techniques one must acquire. Embedded within *craft* are the notions of levels of skill, apprenticeship and mastery, at the service of a defined end.

But as I have said, the actual use of the craft lecture may address the craftless story, consider its formlessness as well as consider the subject of its inspiration while being inspirational at the same time. And I say amen to that.

This kind of craft lecture may provide the only space in a creative writing curriculum where philosophical and conceptual ideas may be discussed. The workshop (for a second, consider the implications just in the name *workshop*) is especially ill equipped to handle a work of fiction whose subject and theme is, say, fiction itself.

Consider the silence generated by, say, a story (irreal, nonnarrative) where a green-skinned woman named Lizard gets drunk and has a fight with her lesbian lover, narrated by a narrator who can't figure out what is going on in his own story and who stops talking about the characters, in any case, and writes an essay on love. Mr. Barthelme, we say, um, this is different. But how do we make this better? How do we tighten, polish, revise, or edit? Is this even a piece of furniture? The form, in these kinds of stories, is in play. And a story such as this will always resist the tweaking of the received form the workshop is designed to craft.

In my lectures on the craft of fiction I have talked about the architecture of Frank Gehry and Richard Rogers and their aesthetic of ruins; the history, utility, and theory of camouflage and its relationship to art and creativity; the narrative design of Depression-era post office murals; and the connection between the Mafia, collage, and Derrida.

In this craft lecture on craft lectures, I talked about chairs.

My point is this: surely in all the talking and thinking done on the art and craft of fiction, some of it can be about it by not being about it. Stories and the writing of them are the record and residue of the imagination in play. A space can be made among the tasks of craft to go off task, a space for the space and for, well, the spacey. The craft lecture allows for the metaphorical as well as the meticulous, the analogical as well as the logical instruction, a place next to the workshop with its relentless efficiency, its attention to certain detail, and its need to regulate and maintain the particulars of form and formula.

Down the road from Swannanoa and Warren Wilson (where I have presented many craft lectures) on the Blue Ridge Parkway there is a little craft store that displays and sells products of Appalachia. Every time I work at Warren Wilson, I visit the store and buy a birdhouse. Some of them are magnificently crafted, indeed little houses, displaying all the skill evident in a well-built human house. Some of the houses look like anything but houses—just beautiful junk arranged with some intelligence, with a perch and hole sometimes added, it seems, as an afterthought. I put all of these habitats in my backyard and wait, watch the birds arrive on their migrations. I never know upon which porch they will alight, in which houses they will build their nests, which perch will be the seat of their singing.

hose Story Is It?

FRAMING THE FRAME OR WRITING BAD ON PURPOSE PURPOSELY

Lex Williford organized a panel that asked the above question for the 1996 AWP convention held in Atlanta. The paper was later published in the *Writer's Chronicle*.

I have my students write bad stories. It is, of course, very hard to do, perhaps even more difficult than writing (as they assume they are doing most of the time) good stories. That is to say, it goes without saying that a workshop is about producing a good story. Assigning the task of creating a bad story actually makes the transparency of the default assignment (you are to write a good story) readily apparent. To ask for the bad in a workshop is a way to confront what is meant by the good. And shouldn't it be easier to write bad since we usually are trying so hard to avoid bad writing as if it is our natural and fallen state?

The solutions to the problem most often generated by the students are good "bad" writing. A convention or rule of thumb is selected, say that one should use active verbs or be specific, and then the bad writing is a satire or parody of this or that craft proscription. In effect, the writer does not create bad writing but creates an imaginary bad writer who then makes the "mistake." What is interesting to see in this bad writing are the methods the writers employ to signal that the writing is consciously bad, not just plain bad, thereby communicating to the reader the goodness of the creator behind the badness of the text. And if the intent of the writing is clear, even if the intent is to be bad, then it will be read as good, as a good piece of writing.

Recently one student appropriated her own writing, bringing in as an example of the bad a selection from a journal she kept when she was ten. After reading it, we all agreed there was something bad about it and that it was a different kind of bad than the parodies and satires of that day. But, I suggested, if the very same writing had been used in a story offered during a regular workshop, a workshop of "good going to better" stories, in which the narrator is a ten-year-old girl and her narrative is in the form of the journal or diary, our response would be the opposite. We would praise the writer now for the fidelity and the realistic texture of the prose. "This is good," we would say. "This sounds just like the diary of a ten-year-old girl."

I have been thinking about the issue of framing stories and especially how the workshop itself acts as a frame. Most narratives I see in my workshops are from the point of view of an amateur, often inarticulate, narrator who struggles to narrate a crucial moment in a personal or private history. These stories are in the form of the mock memoir or the mock biography. What makes them good is not the writing per se but the success of their realism, their apparent spontaneity, and the artful artlessness of their construction. Writers struggle very hard to make these stories seem to have simply happened. They must seem blurted out. When written in the first person, these stories appear best when they appear to be mere transcriptions of an impassioned utterance. This, of course, is realism's game, that the apparatus of its construction is completely hidden. But in order for this artful artlessness to be read as artful artfulness at all, the story must be framed as art. The workshop is that frame. The presentation of such stories in a workshop allows these seemingly spontaneous narratives to show forth as art.

A frame, then, renders the story, in some ways, safe. We can read it as a story and not have to confront its content solely. We can read it as a confession of a rape *and* a pretend confession, for instance. Or another story presents us with an explanation of adultery *and* the awareness that it is a made-up explanation of adultery. The anxiety of the reader is relieved; a distance is created. The workshop is very good at disarming or exposing the story's camouflage, so good that its function as a frame is rarely or never, I've found, discussed. The workshop proceeds as a given, and we are meant to forget its very complex function as a context in which we read. By ignoring the workshop as a fictional frame, we miss teaching our students about the artistic manipulation of the frame. We concentrate on the object on the table, the stories, and ignore the table they are on.

I have been very interested recently in creating fictions that pass as the real thing. I have published a fictional travel guide called *The Blue Guide to Indiana,* parts of which have passed as actual travel writing in an Indiana newspaper. Also, I have "written" several stories in which I have not written a word. That is, I have appropriated completely other texts, both in public domain and in copyright, and through the arrangement and the framing of those texts published them as original.

I am, after all, a fiction writer, and I bring up the notion of passing here because it makes self-consciously clear the business I am involved in. Counterfeiter and liar, manipulator of texts and voice, stealer of experience.

These fictions of my own, I admit, are a bit extreme. They are fictions about the act of fiction making. I invoke them here in order to call attention to this other aspect of my role as producer of art. I am not simply the creator of objects but also the creator of the contexts in which those objects are created and displayed, in which they show forth and do work.

I sense a complacency, an indifference, about the contexts—the workshop, the university, all forms of publishing—in which I teach fiction writing and fiction making and in which I present my fiction and the fiction of others. In workshop, we workshop stories but seldom turn our critical eye toward reading the workshop.

It is easy to forget about the frame of the workshop, to think of it (if we think of it at all) as a benign occasion, a neutral space where the real work, the stories, are considered. But the workshop, I am saying, is itself a kind of fiction.

So here is my answer to the question: Whose story is it? A story, in a workshop, is the workshop's story.

The careful creator of fiction should also always be conscious of the frame of the story as well as the story itself. The setting of the fictional object, its framing, is a significant contributor to the meaning of a piece. The control of the frame should be as much, if not more so, a subject of our study and an object of our craft.

ygmies Dressed as Pygmies

W. Scott Olsen asked me to write on travel writing for the 2002 AWP convention in New Orleans. He then published the piece in *Ascent*, the magazine he edits.

"I don't know, what do you want to do?" So begins an amazing scene recorded in *The Forest People*, an anthropological record of African forest pygmies Colin Turnbull lived with for several years. These forest people, as you might guess, were hunter-gatherers living in primeval jungle. Groups such as these also traded with people of a nearby agricultural settlement on the forest's edge, their connection with the larger world. On what was a long pygmy weekend, Turnbull is sitting around with his informants as they discuss the impending leisure time.

"I don't know, what do you want to do?"

"Don't ask me. What do you want to do?"

"There's nothing to do. What do you want to do?"

It is a scene right out of *Marty* and written in such a way as to say, see, these folks are not that much different from you or me, bored as we are with the distractions of our small lives. Suddenly one of the group jumps up with a brilliant idea. "I know," he says, "let's get dressed up like pygmies, go down to the village, and let the tourists take our pictures." And that's what they do. Attiring themselves with feathers and paint and weaponry, they wander off to the village, looking very primitive and untouched by the civilization that will now record that fact with cameras.

Today, I am thinking about the tourists of this scene. The ones waiting, also probably bored (I don't know, what do you want to do?). They find themselves in this village waiting with cameras and tape recorders for the possible arrival of a "real" thing to happen, a "real" event they will be able to document. That is one reason to travel, isn't it, to get out and experience something other than what we are so conscious of, so self-conscious of, something so different from our humanly constructed forest of what we once called man-made existence—these artifices we manufacture and consume, these massaged simulations we call life that somehow don't seem like real life.

But there is another tourist in this scene, of course, Turnbull himself, the writer, who in writing photographs the scene. In fact there are actual photographs reproduced in his book that Turnbull has taken—pictures of tourists taking pictures of pygmies dressed up as pygmies. The scene in the book is presented as a discovery of the real real event—the behind-the-scenes production of the dramatic production performed for the tourists down at the village. Turnbull gets to be the real tourist. He gets to see the pygmies in their natural habitat, so to speak, and the tourists in theirs.

The reader, too, is a kind of tourist and also gets access to the real life of the pygmies with Turnbull's mediation. I, the tourist reader, can think of myself smugly, better than those saps, the tourists of the book waiting down at the village. I have the backstage pass. I know the skinny. I possess the knowledge of the back story, the story behind the story. My journey into the world of the forest people is better, more authentic, than those who have actually journeyed there. I have seen the unvarnished truth, have actually witnessed the varnishing of truth, as the pygmies turn themselves into pygmies.

Of course, this sensation I have as I read, the experience that I have actually experienced an authentic moment, is itself an illusion. I am reading it in a book. I have never actually physically been to Africa, let alone anywhere near that part of Africa where one finds the forest people. My journey has been to a destination created in a book. It seems very real. It seems very, very real. It has stuck with me for years. I read this first as a freshman in college. It is real enough that I believe this scene of pygmies dressing as pygmies and tourists acting like tourists has actually happened. But has it? Do you, the audience for this paper, believe it when I tell you this happened? This event today, this paper, is another man-made environment, isn't it? Another simulation? Pygmies dressing up like pygmies. Tourists dressing up like tourists. Anthropologists dressing up as anthropologists. Writers dressing up as writers. Readers dressing up as readers. You dressing up as you.

I was born in Fort Wayne, Indiana, in 1955. That same year the Eisenhower administration launched the Defense Highway Act, the interstate highway system, with the vision that one day one would travel by car coast-to-coast without ever encountering a stoplight. But what would one encounter? Travel to where? That same year, Disneyland opened in California, and the first McDonald's hamburger stand opened in Illinois, initiating the transformation in the landscape that I think we sometimes see as world of creation (which we see as real, valuable) becoming a world of recreation (which we regard with suspicion, a simulation). That is, we have a sense that, only recently, in my lifetime, large economic, media, and governmental forces have driven out of this world the more authentic world and left us hungry for what is real.

I went to graduate school in Baltimore, and late at night after fiction workshops my classmates and I would travel down to the Inner Harbor, where only a few months before, the skipjacks of the Chesapeake oyster fleet, the last fishing fleet still under real sail, landed their catch and where the McCormick spice factory vented the aroma of all those spices it had collected from all over the world as it processed, dried, crushed, and shredded the seeds, barks, and flowers, masking the reek of the water, the fish, the produce being transported by Arabers, black men driving carts pulled by ponies culled from the wild herds of Chincoteague Island. The odor was so strange, so foreign, so marvelous to a boy from the Midwest. But that had been a few months before. Now a new mall was being built—Harborplace—that would, when completed, display pictures of the harbor it had displaced and suggest in its advertising that if you came to this place you would experience a bit of that lost authentic world. The McCormick plant until recently remained after the mall opened, still scenting the harbor now that it had transformed from a wholesale to retail landscape with the same seasonings of the Far East, the fields of Provence, the rain forests, India, the whole alphabet of seasonings.

Still, you feel something has changed, something not quite right. Is it as simple as the move from the wholesaling to the retailing of experience? The crabs on the docks have somehow transformed while remaining crabs. We don't simply eat them. We now have an aesthetic sense that we are eating them. In fact it doesn't even seem we have to eat anything anymore. We don't eat merely to survive. We choose to eat now and choose how we eat, not so much a creative act as a recreational one. We choose to eat crabs in this manner, in the "authentic" way, a pile of them, all steamed, whacking them with the "authentic" wooden mallet, a table covered with the "authentic" brown butcher paper, on the "authentic" shore of this "authentic" harbor.

Bastard quotation marks buzz around us as we eat like these "real" flies that buzz around us as we eat. We are no longer simply eating but seeing ourselves as "eating." Are we conscious now that we consume the experience of consuming instead of simply experiencing experience? Perhaps we still hunger for the unmediated experience? Perhaps we pretend, when we have these highly mediated experiences, that they are in fact "real." We forget to remember we are performing the role of the consumer. We forget we are tourists dressed up like tourists. We can, we believe, just eat.

But perhaps the self-conscious feeling of feeling is not new, has always been the case. The Seven Wonders of the Ancient World, you remember, were all man-made destinations, constructed things, the malls of their day. The church manufactured the pilgrimages of the Dark Ages; think of them as a kind of Elderhostel. The Crusades were a kind of group tour of the Holy Land, especially the Children's Crusade, where the tour guides got a huge kickback from the merchants of Constantinople. And then there are the guidebooks themselves. One may read Herodotus and Pausanias not that much differently from our contemporary guidebooks. That is to say, they record and promote destinations almost exclusively of humanly massaged and constructed places, often places — theaters, temples, stadia — constructed by natives to stage their own constructed imaginary scenes, rituals, and reenactments of real things. There is also, in those guidebooks, that tone we are so aware of today. It is that tone promising you that here in these pages is the real dope, the important stuff, no kidding, no fooling. These are insider guides, off-the-beaten-path guides. You can be like the native. Even back then, the real, the authentic, the actual were so elusive, just over the next hill, just out of reach. In this book are the tips to find the last unspoiled landscape, the virgin view, the undiscovered discovery.

Perhaps, just perhaps, the world was never real. It has always been an artifice, a giant theme park, and our travel has always been an elaborate invention of our own making, an entertaining ride of our own invention.

I think it's very funny that mostly I have read the great travel books as the books I read as I travel. I remember specifically reading Henry Miller's *The Colossus of Maroussi*, where Miller travels to Epidarus and experiences the heartbeat of the world, while sitting in the theater there. The day I was at Epidarus to listen for the heartbeat, the place was packed with people, many of them, like me, reading dog-eared and broken-spined editions of *The Colossus of Maroussi*. Hundreds of people down on the stage were yelling up to their friends in the theater's farthest rows, to check the remarkable acoustics, while just as many other people milled about, looking at the site through the viewfinders of their cameras, angling for the moment when no other people, also looking through their cameras, appeared in the viewfinder, so they could snap a picture of a theater, a ruin, deserted, pristine, unself-conscious, authentic, real.

You have had the experience of traveling so far and with so much effort to a place you, until this moment, have only read about, only to discover the actual place so diminished compared to the actual place you first visited in your reading now lodged in your head. It is like returning to the neighborhood where you were a child only to find it shrunken, colorless, wholly obvious that, as a place, it isn't remotely worth the memories you've made of it.

Perhaps writing about the world spoils the world for the writer and the reader. Or more precisely, if reading and writing don't really spoil the world, they do spoil the way we want to experience the world, as unspoiled, when we are not reading or writing about it. Our writing and reading get in the way of our actual adventures. As actual adventures, writing and reading substitute remarkably for actual actual adventures. No frigate like a book. I believe there is a real world out there, but I suspect, more and more, that I am ill equipped to capture it, to perceive it, to record it, to even recognize it. My sensing apparatus, my brain, my nerves are just not calibrated to receive the real real. This is especially true when other humans, so equipped and so motivated, are out there, too, mucking it up, trying to make sense of this, this very made and very made-up world.

One final anecdote. *Foxfire* is a series, perhaps seven or eight by now, of books collecting the folkways and crafts of the people in Appalachia. The folklorists who published the first edition were surprised by its huge success so went on to other parts of the region to collect more intelligence on basket weaving, furniture making, music, home remedies, and the like. As they traveled, the authors were amazed and very happy at the variety they found in each local culture, publishing many volumes, recording everything new they discovered. At last after a decade, they returned to their original informants and were shocked to find these people had abandoned their ancient methods and traditional crafts. They were now making baskets similar to those being made three states away. "What happened?" they asked. "Why are you making your baskets like this?" The informants, who were quite proud of their new baskets and who liked the new baskets a whole lot better than the old ones they had been making, answered the folklorists by bringing out an old, worn book obviously studied, handled by the whole community. It was *Foxfire 4*. "We found this book," they said.

# The Tyranny of Praise

This paper was delivered at the 1997 AWP convention in Washington, D.C. The meeting was held in a hotel near my favorite museum in the city, the National Museum of American Art, where once-popular art is housed away from the museums on the Mall.

I was standing in line waiting to use an outdoor ATM built into the wall of the Schine, the student activity center at Syracuse University, where I used to teach. Waiting behind me was a colleague, a poet, from the creative writing program, and I turned to talk with him. It was spring, a truly lovely and rare couple of minutes in the yearlong perpetual gloom that the lake effect generates. So there I was. And there was sunlight, a bit of warmth, maybe even some birds chirping. And I turn to remark upon this fact to my colleague standing behind me in line when I catch sight for the first time of a new installation of outdoor art covering the lawn of a building two hundred yards away.

Now, I had read about this work, a group of twenty or so sculptures, fiberglass or resin, I think, sculptures of women, larger than life-size, naked, arranged in a kind of Stonehenge circle, frozen in various contorted gestures of grief and mourning. They were modeled on the mothers of Syracuse University students killed in the bombing of Pam Am flight 103, which had crashed five years before. The sculptor, a mother herself, whose son had died on the flight, asked the others to recreate the moment they had understood their child had died, that first sharp intake of breath. And I caught my breath seeing the grouping for the first time, even though I had read about the work, looking over the shoulder of my colleague to the greening lawn and the figures shimmering and quaking on the hillside in the rare sunlight among the living people walking there. And my colleague seeing me so struck turned, following my gaze to gaze at the collection of sculpture and then said something quite amazing. "You know," he said, "it's moving but it is not great art."

Now it may be the case that the sculpture may not be great art. It probably is the case. I don't really know and don't really care one way or the other. What struck me that moment and what has stayed with me since that moment was the need my colleague expressed, the need to make such a judgment. Or, put another way, what struck me is that judgment would be the initial response, that he would be driven to begin the culling, begin constructing the scaffolding of hierarchy, that he would find it necessary to establish his position as being in the position to make such a definitive determination.

Let's muse for a second on how writers find themselves in the role of judge, arbiter of taste, gatekeeper of the good.

I entered my first teaching job at Iowa State University the object of a terminal-degree war where enlightened colleagues (in my view) in the English Department were arguing for my inclusion though I held only the lowly MA. I began teaching quite conscious of my status as not quite professorial to some while at the same time aware that I owed what status I did have to my PhDed betters, some of whom were willing to share at least some crumbs of the table. Better be on my best behavior. Since no one I worked with saw me as a professor in the usual sense, I had to be more professor than professors.

Not a new story. Walker Percy in *Love in the Ruins* has a religious black character say to an ambivalent white one: "You know what really bothers you is that we out-jesused you." One way to read James Joyce is as an Irish revenge on the language of the oppressor. He out-Englished the English. So I was primed to out-profess the professor.

And look! That anxiety is replicated in the organization that gathers us here. The AWP, since I have been in it, has been driven to shape up the writer as some sort of professional professional, insisting on the trappings of accreditation and rank, etc. And, by the way, my MA credential, according to what my professional organization preaches, is not a terminal degree, so officially I am, once again, underqualified, policed by my own. At Warren Wilson College I am also quite conscious of that program's insistence on standards, qualifications, and curricular rigor. It is the overcompensation brought on by the severe institutional gaze, an institution deeply involved with gradation, rank, hierarchy, credentialization. Man, what we must do when we are looking to pass as professors.

On one hand, then, we felt the heat to shape up, and up we shaped, not only adopting the Burberry and Volvo camouflage of the class but internalizing and then exaggerating the critical impulse, adopting the caretaker status of the beautiful and the good as professors are e'er to do. Paradoxically or perhaps logically, as we out-professored the professors, the dons in lit crit headed for territories, leaving us the ruins of literature. Our audience, too, our young students, everybody perhaps, seemed to have been moving on as well.

As writers in universities took on the roles of role models, those roles, according to our betters and lessers (now that we see the world in such terms), weren't even in the script anymore. What's a boy to do? Well one response is to cling even harder to the hard-earned function of fiduciary trusteeship. "It's not art!" And when no one else is teaching the matter you worked so hard to master (MA or MFA), insist with all the might of your position that Catullus is still a must.

So what kind of classroom may be generated by those who were themselves generated by a culture of righteous discrimination? It may become a brutal place where one applies the honed edge of his displayed credentials as writer and teacher to define and prioritize the work of inferiors, to create a Darwinian landscape of competition in which, as one of my teachers said in class one day, "This poem beats up on this poem." The models are boot camp or medical internship, in which the main lesson is not simply to know one's place but to internalize that the concept of "place" exists in the first place. The landscape of judgment, however, is not exclusively the purview of the sadist or survivalist. Don't you know the moment when students desperately seek to ameliorate the damage they have been allowed to inflict on their silent colleague, the one who is "up," when they say, well we have been critical, now let's say what works about this piece? The kiss is substituted for the club, but the underlying ideology remains in place. This workshop is a platform upon which work becomes "better," and what "better" means is known by the teacher who had it clubbed or kissed into him or her, who makes his or her students work for it.

This is the grammar lesson of cheerleading, the declension of coaching. But it is still part of a landscape of judgment. Praise, encouragement, positive reinforcement, reward, incentive. They are all of the same ilk as ridicule, sarcasm, punishment, and anger. They emanate out of the same model, which is that teaching is about modifying behavior, motivating proper behavior, a behavior that is known but to the teacher.

Allow me to introduce you to the work of Alfie Kohn, author of *No Contest, The Case against Competition,* and *Punished by Rewards: The Trouble with Gold Stars, Incentive Plans, A's, Praise, and other Bribes.* Kohn takes to task the shallow behaviorist model of human nature by deploying behaviorists' own studies to demonstrate that motivation techniques do not work and in fact often achieve the exact opposite effect initially desired. Elementary reading programs, for example, that reward readers with pizzas actually destroy the desire to read by making reading a means to an end instead of allowing reading to be intrinsically rewarding. Many writing students report to me that they don't like the act of writing as much as they once did. Now they are far more interested in being recognized as being a writer by their workshop teacher. Classically, according to Kohn, they are not hooked on writing but hooked on praise. Workshops, then, are not about teaching writing but about teaching how to teach workshops. As Kohn points out, when the work of a high-status person is praised by a low-status one, the praise is often seen as insulting precisely because praise itself implies *first* a difference of position—the most notable aspect of a positive judgment is not that it is positive but that it is a *judgment*. And the reaction is either to aspire to the position of judgment or to repudiate the whole business.

And that's what I say: The heck with it. I believe in the intrinsic desire of people to write and reject the notion they must be made to do so. I can recognize the work as good without asserting my power to crown the work "good" with the thorny superior punctuation of my quotation.

Welcome to Baltimore (aka) Charm City (colon):

A CHARM BRACELET OF HALF-BAKED DELICACIES,
OR
XENOPHON'S *ANABASIS* AND THE COLLAPSE OF THE AVANT-GARDE
INTO WAVES OF ECSTASY

I delivered a second paper at the 2003 AWP convention in Baltimore. "Welcome to Baltimore" was part of a panel on the avant-garde put together by R. M. Berry, publisher of FC2 and professor at Florida State University. The piece was republished on-line at the *Electronic Book Review*. I was reading Xenophon as the country was preparing for war in Iraq, the setting for the military adventure chronicled in the *Anabasis*.

There's an epigraph:

(A motto or quotation, as at the beginning of a literary composition, setting forth a theme. [Greek, *epigraph*, to write on]—*American Heritage Dictionary of the English Language*)

> Hey, Rock, watch me pull a rabbit out of my hat!
> BULLWINKLE J. MOOSE

The GI Bill Considered as the Indian Removal Act

What brings us to Baltimore? We can thank a forward-looking piece of legislation at the end of a war, the GI Bill, as the material impetus for moving this art of writing into the university — for our university affiliation, the professionalization of our activity, the tribal organization of our guild, the expected enaction of academic ritual as expressed by conventions. Voilà: Baltimore. The story of the literary artist and art and its now sixty-year integration with an institution founded in the Middle Ages would be an interesting story if I had time or if that were the task. Instead, consider this: this culture has been successful at impounding its artists in a kind of reservation. The university provides an inoculation frame, a context in order to order, to control, to make sense. This gathering? Have we rabbited from our reservations? Have we escaped the context of this definition? Baltimore is a port city. This convention may be considered our island of quarantine.

The Avant-Garde Taken Literally, as Expressed in Xenophon's *Anabasis,* or *The March Up Country,* the Rouse Translation

From Book Four: They reached the mountain on the fifth day. When the first men reached the summit and caught sight of the sea there was loud shouting. Xenophon and the rear guard, hearing this, thought that more enemies were attacking in front. . . . But when the shouts grew louder and nearer, as each group came up it went pelting along to the shouting men in front, and the shouting was louder and louder as the crowds increased. Xenophon thought it must be something very important; he mounted his horse and galloped to bring help forward. As he rode he heard the soldiers shouting "Sea! Sea!" and passing the word along in waves.

Derrida Consumed by Crabs

1966. Derrida arrives in Baltimore, twenty-nine city blocks north of where we are now, to deliver, for the first time on these shores, the obituary of the author at the very moment the construction of authorship in America is evolving from the romantic individual genius to the romantic individual genius with tenure. Later Derrida is taken to a crab house on Belair Road where he is instructed in the procedure for disassembling the steamed Maryland blue crab. He is a quick study. He becomes proficient at removing the carapace, the feathery lungs and mustard some consider a delicacy, adept at cracking the claws with knife and wooden mallet, extracting the lump meat from the compartments of cartilage. The flesh of the crab is like soap. The act of consuming consumes him.

Why Do We Eat Human Flesh?

Some of us eat human flesh and drink human blood. Weekly. We do so in the context of the Christian faith, in the setting of the church. Art too is framed deviance. If the avant-garde is regarded as a transgressive movement, can it transgress the frame that makes it art? Is that, in fact, the only transgression left to transgress? The *Catechism of the Catholic Church* in America was written in Baltimore, Maryland, the Roman Catholic reservation. A catechism is a book that gives a brief summary of basic principles in question and answer form. Is there a brief summary of basic principles, a catechism, for the avant-garde? Can art ask questions that have answers? Can it exist outside the picket fencing of its own inquisition? Must art be art? Must flesh transubstantiate in order to be consumed?

The Women's Industrial Exchange

on Charles Street dates from the nineteenth century, when it was founded to provide women a means to market the fruits of their domestic labor. There one can still purchase handicrafts—clothing, ceramics, paper ephemera, decoupage, lace and linens, millinery, jewelry, quilts, and souvenirs—as well as consumables—baked goods, preserves, candies, and herbs and spices. There is a tearoom too. The Women's Industrial Exchange excites me! The building is a kind of portal. It even had its own doorman until his recent retirement. A portal that indeed leads back to the past, but more importantly, a portal where the products of anonymous artists appear spontaneously to then be consumed by the visitor. True, the art that materializes on Charles Street is not of the genres we would here today recognize as the art of the avant-garde. But its delivery system is for me current. Art that appears. Art that is found. Devoid of signature. My favorites are pieces of utility that have been transformed into the useless or the useless made into the useful — bread dough baked and glazed with silicon, then affixed with googly eyes and magnets — the utilitarian on the verge of metamorphosing into art. This is like finding a Duchamp in Baltimore but without the baggage of "Duchamp," a museum nowhere near, ready-mades without the anointment of Art. The Women's Industrial Exchange takes us back to this future.

The Row House of Gertrude Stein Is For Sale
The Row House of Gertrude Stein Is For Sale
The Row House of Gertrude Stein Is For Sale

Once when looking for an apartment in Baltimore, I found an ad in the classified section of the *Sun* offering for sale in the Druid Hill neighborhood a row house once owned and occupied by Gertrude Stein. This caught my attention. Perhaps the most interesting aspect of the notice was the authorial assumption that by informing the reader that the row house was once owned and occupied by Gertrude Stein this would, in fact, be a selling point as persuasive as the parquet floors and the mahogany banister, the leaded windows and the renovated kitchen. I had a chance once to purchase the house where, it was advertised by the seller, Raymond Carver wrote the short story "Cathedral." Or was it the house where what happens in the short story "Cathedral" happened? Either way, the space was promoted as valuable, as though these actions, the writing about something or the something that the writing was about, now dust, no, not even dust but something simply over and gone, had, in the end, coin, had added value in the calculation of real real estate. How curious this perceived desire to inhabit the habitation of a name, to possess the apostrophe of another's possession. "Gertrude Stein" as brand is known how? She wrote all those words, all those books of words, ordered all those words and all those books in order to construct a phrase or two that would stick, that stuck, that infected the reader, that reordered his or her own row house of DNA, own chemical charm bracelet of memory. "A rose is a rose is a rose" is a kind of row house block. See the optical illusion of the foreshortened front porches as you look down the street! The repetition of the marble stoops. The repetition of the painted screen doors. "There is no there there" was the epigraph of my thesis written in Baltimore, Maryland, in a row house on Charles Street, before I saw the ad in the *Sun* offering for sale the row house once owned and occupied by Gertrude Stein, before it had even been written, had even been thought to be written. Gertrude Stein wrote "There is no there there," it is said, about Oakland, California. I associated "There is no there there" with Fort Wayne, Indiana. I am reading this to an audience in a hotel in Baltimore, Maryland. I have no idea where or in what house Gertrude Stein wrote "There is no there there," but I suspect that it was as true there as well, as meaningful or not there too, that there there was no there there.

The Westernmost Eastern City; the Southernmost Northern City; the Easternmost Western City; the Northernmost Southern City

Baltimore! When I was thinking of moving here to go to graduate school, I talked to George Starbuck, who wanted me to move to Boston instead. He said: "You don't want to go to Baltimore. It is the world's largest small town." Perhaps this art thing is not about transgression but about the situating of the whole idea of art and one's art, of one's art between the spaces, on the lines. Not so much the breaking of boundaries, but the inscription of elaborate Venn diagrams on the culture. The waves of overlap instead of the tide rising. Not the context of no context but the context of context alone.

Martone Consumed by Crabs

The summer before Harborplace opened, Martone wandered down to the Inner Harbor of Baltimore in the hope of capturing what coolness there was in the city. Looking into the water, Martone discovered an infestation of the harbor by crabs, doublers in fact, crabs in the act of mating. The salinity of the bay was such as to allow the crustaceans rare access to this most often sweet inlet of the massive estuary. The Latin name for the blue crab translates thus: beautiful swimmer: delicious. There were millions of them, doubled, making millions more. The articulation of their graceful motion through the water. The architecture of their passion. The narrative of their cheap horror-movie choreography. It was envy he felt, envy that the anonymous phenomenon of Baltimore in its display had again been more imaginative than he, a trained professional.

Xenophon, in Retreat with His Army through Present-Day Turkey, Races to the Front, Fearing the Worst

But they had made it out alive. There it was. The way back home to Greece. The men in the vanguard were shouting "Sea! Sea!" which in Greek is pronounced "Thalasa! Thalasa!" Onomatopoeia. The sound of the waves of the sea crashing over Xenophon as he, the leader of this disastrous exposition and the historian of the same, charged to the front. "Sea! Sea!" In English, a homophone. Going forward in retreat. To be swamped by human language, to be consumed by it, its ecstatic reaction to the steady static of the world.

The Constellation Is Not the Constellation; The Constitution Is Not the Constitution: Frigates Considered as Vehicles Embodying Change

The USS Constellation currently undergoing renovation on display in Baltimore's Inner Harbor is not one of the six original frigates of the U.S. Navy. What you see is the remnant of a later ship of the same name built to fight slave trading in the 1850s, an interesting story but one suppressed in favor of the fiction of origin for commercial touristic reasons. The USS Constitution in Boston is the oldest commissioned warship in the world. The oldest commissioned warship except that through renovation none of the original survives. The eighteenth-century ship you observe has been completely consumed by its own maintaining. It is timeful and timeless. It is hard to regard these ships, these floating fabrications of stories, as works of art. We try to make sense of them as we eat our crab cake sandwiches. We consider their wood sides transformed, we recall, to iron sides by means of a poem, a poem that saved the ship from scrap. We regard the complication of their riggings while we savor our crab cakes, crab cakes not made of crab but pollack, dyed and flavored to be crab.

The Aesthetic of the Half-Baked: The Maryland Beaten Biscuit

I apologize for this bracelet of false starts, postcards all captioned with little message save this: "Wish you were here." And here you are. I am both a producer and consumer of art, and the art I produce mostly consumes other art. The metaphor the avant-garde maintains is that there is a difference between production and consumption, the performer and the audience, you and me. I am here to tell you that these distinctions are not distinct for me. There is not the world and the art of the world. Artifice is all and its arrangement the lookout of us all in both of those roles. I offer these half-baked ideas, not even ideas. Notes, then. Notes of notes. Half-baked notions on the notion of notion. I am here suggesting the aesthetic of the TV dinner, the precooked and flash-frozen, the heat and serve, the shake and bake, the poppin' fresh, the just add water, the just add meat, the process of the processed, the condensed and reconstituted, the prepackaged, the some assembly required. I am the maker of parts made of the wholes. The recipe for the Maryland Beaten Biscuit, a kind of hardtack, an Eastern Shore delicacy, is this: flour, salt, butter, and milk to make a stiff dough, and a hatchet. Mix and beat for thirty minutes—preferably on a tree stump—until all the air is removed and the dough blisters. One hot, typically swampy, humid summer in Baltimore, I had a hankering for some beaten biscuits. One place to get them here in town is the Women's Industrial Exchange. I asked the woman behind the counter for some beaten biscuits. She told me they didn't have any. "Hon," she said, "it's too hot to beat."

My Situation

Gordon Hunter of the journal *American Literary History* asked twenty-six writers to respond to a series of questions he posed for a symposium he titled "The Situation of American Writing 1999." What follows is my response.

For the last few years I have been writing fictions that attempt to pass as nonfictions. I recently published a book called *The Blue Guide to Indiana*, which is a fake travel guide. Passages from the book have been published in Indiana newspapers as actual reporting, feature articles on what to do this weekend or suggestions for family vacations. These pieces are published without any indication that they are made up (bogus history, invented places, false directions, etc.) and I have attempted, with all my skill, to make the particulars seem plausible. The audience, then, is a general newspaper-reading one who, I assume, is reading the fiction in the context of fact.

I got to this place as an extension of my previous work. I realize I have never written stories in a technical sense. On many occasions I employed "real" people as narrators (the swimmer Mark Spitz is a narrator, as are Harlan Sanders, Alfred Kinsey, James Dean's high school drama teacher, and Dan Quayle) who would, usually in a monologue, compose a kind of essay. I wrote fake essays, then, in the fictional voices of actual people. In all this work, I was always interested in the relationship between fact and fiction as well as the nuances at play in a culture of celebrity and fame saturated with many narrative delivery devices. For me it was about the constructions of character in the midst of a culture in which construction of character and narrative was an active business enterprise and cultural phenomenon.

Perhaps the end result of these experiments with character was the publication of *Pensées: The Thoughts of Dan Quayle*, a collection of twelve fictional essays written by my "Dan Quayle" and published in a format that looked very much like Mao's *Thoughts*, his *Little Red Book*, which my book, a little gray one, mimicked in design. *The Thoughts of Dan Quayle* appeared on the very same day Dan Quayle published his "own" ghostwritten "memoir" to spark his presidential ambitions. I published my book in Indianapolis, and the newspaper there, owned by Quayle's family, was doing a Citizen Kane on Dan's book. It was being covered in the *Star* as a news story, reviewed as a book, politically editorialized, reported on in the business section, featured as human interest, etc. Mention of my book, I was delighted to discover, appeared not as a book review but as a sidebar on the front page, an interesting news item. Here, the reporter reported, is this curious other book by Dan.

The result of this is that I now think of the work I do more as the making of things, of objects, instead of simply the generation of text. I would like these artifacts to then more or less modulate the stream of dreaming that is present in our collective consumption of narrative everywhere. I am more conscious and desire more control of the complete package and presentation of my written work as a means to insert my bit of code within all the other coding going on. I don't only want to create the written text but to have a hand in the creation of the frame, the context in which it appears. I want to create the delivery vehicle as well.

More and more I think of these fictions as viral. That is, they are designed to infect the memory of the reader, any reader. The traditional contexts of presentations of literary texts (literary magazines, commercial book publishers, genre distinctions in bookstores) for me now seem to be means of rendering writing safe for consumption by readers who are to know their place as readers. There may, when one knowingly reads a novel or short story, still be a willing suspension of disbelief, but those frames allow for the stereoscopic consciousness: I believe this though I know it is made up.

I'm now in for a penny, in for a pound. If I am a fiction writer, I am going to create fictions that do not in any way say they are fiction. Fiction as fiction. Fiction as totally camouflaged fact. The big fiction.

I was very happy when I received a call from a reporter working for the *Washington Post*. I had published an article from *The Blue Guide* concerning a series of tourist sites connected to death in Indiana (The Tomb of Orville Redenbacher, The Bronze Mortuary at the Cemetery at Naked City, The National Monument for Those Killed by Tornadoes in Trailer Parks and Mobile Home Courts, and The Federal Research and Testing Center for Coffin and Casket Standards), and the reporter told me he was doing a story about little-known federal facilities and had heard about the federal testing of coffins. Could I direct him there? Why, yes, I could.

It seems interesting, then, to place before an audience fiction that is designed to add to the unease of the moment, the bombardment of the perception with juxtaposed data. "Is this real or not?" I look to have a response that is broader than appreciation. "What a good story!" "It is a Best American Story!" I like to believe that my fictions are doing some other kind of work in the world. They work to reveal the way framing works and who controls the frame. I no longer want to spend my time solving the puzzle of perfecting the details of received literary conventions.

It is a great time to be or to want to be this kind of satirist. The means of production (computers, copying, printing) is relatively cheap and widely available. The cultural message to poets and writers of literary fiction is clear: cold storage in universities and/ or a narrow and narrowing band of traditional publishing, reviewing, and distributing occasions for you guys. We live, we are told continuously, in an information age. Writers are invited to think of themselves in the conventional role of producers of raw material, material that is easily categorized as literary fiction and ignored or is then processed by larger collaborative concerns (book publishing, movies, television, magazines, etc.) into a value-added product. Or they have an opportunity to become *ronin*, strike out on their own, produce much more of their own work, explore ways to infect the gigantic narrative beast, lay a few eggs under the skin.

It is also a great time to be this kind of satirist as many literary theorists are now paying more attention to these same questions and less to the appreciation of products of traditional genres. Literary theorists are creating their own kind of creative writing and no longer producing literary criticism to explain or translate traditional literary efforts. Good on them! As academic scholarship focuses upon these other things (questions of authorship, cultural commodities, narrative theory), technological innovations (computers, Internet) by their very nature challenge conventions of romantic/modernist authorship, originality, genius, intellectual property, etc. This is a good thing too.

For me this landscape seems exciting, chaotic, and challenging. It also seems liberated from the exhausted desire to impose standards, judgment, and hierarchy. I feel like making things, winding them up and sending them out in the world without the older aesthetic nervousness about quality product for a discerning readership. I am interested in creating curious objects that by their very curious nature force whoever comes across them in whatever context to make a sense out of them.

I like the artist who takes his finished and fired pots, breaks them, and scatters the shards in secret at a construction site to be found later by baffled backhoe operators. I like the fact that my five year old could have drawn that. I think the Museum of Jurassic Technology is a terrific novel. As I mentioned above, I am a satirist in the tradition that extends through the empirical age. I want to dramatize the paradox of belief that all one can know is a product of one's senses at the same time one knows the senses can be so easily misled. The apparatus of story writing, of narrative delivery, of fiction making is what I concentrate on, not the residue of the writing that seeks classic status, canonization, or timelessness.

Creative writing workshops and writing programs seem trapped, spending so much of the time focused on the object on the table without considering its frame (the creative writing workshop, the literary work, the university, etc.) as if the context goes without saying. That is why craft is emphasized, the tweaks of detail and style, as a way of avoiding these larger questions of intent. This piece of writing must be made better, the belief goes, as if what is better can somehow be demonstrated, codified, empirically proved, taught, and then remain consistent for all times and every place.

Having worked in universities for twenty years, I am struck by the shrinking focus of many of my colleagues who write fiction and poetry, who seem to insist more and more on their gatekeeping status and feel so disappointed in the failing standards and quality of the audience. We live in the most leaden age of this age of lead, they seem to wail. I like what the artist Brad Holland had to say of the current situation:

> More than a hundred years ago some French bohemians decreed that the purpose of art was to shock the middle classes. It may have been a great idea back then. But these days the middle classes aren't paying attention. They're all on the Jerry Springer or Ricki Lake show talking about their cross dressing experiences or sex with the baby sitter. Cutting edge artists have to watch this stuff in despair and complain about the state of American culture. . . . In the future this spectacle of the middle classes shocking the avant garde will probably become the textbook definition of Postmodernism.

More than the reversal of roles implied in this statement, I am comfortable with the notion that there is no difference between the producer and consumer of cultural artifacts. I am not simply the writer, and the audience is not simply the other out there. Why should these roles be so passive, so static? I don't think of myself as a writer with insight or one gifted or better attuned than anyone else. I don't mourn the passing of the unacknowledged legislator of the world. I don't miss the guildhall for specialists when the specialty is the language and literacy. I hope that we no longer feel we must ride herd on quality control, police peerage, anoint and promote. I don't write to pass muster. The activity is not a means to that end for me. It's not a test to pass or a means to get an award. Writing seems to me an intrinsic pleasure, an end in itself first. I'm not proprietary about my talent, knowledge, insight, or experience. The question for me is not whether my writing, or any piece of writing, is good or bad but what the writing is and what it is doing and how finally it is used or can be used by others.

Telling Stories Short

In 1985 Kim A. Herzinger convened a symposium for a special issue of *Mississippi Review*, number 40/41. The topic was "On the New Fiction" and the "New Fiction" meant minimalism and whatever that meant. Another essay in the magazine, "A Downpour of Literary Republicanism" by Joe David Bellamy, identifies me as a minimalist. I skirt the issue and concentrate on the *New Yorker* magazine and its curious role as sole purveyor of the "New Fiction."

A few years ago I learned that the *New Yorker* was traded publicly over the counter. I bought a few shares. And over the years, whenever I had a little extra money, I'd buy a few more. All that time I was sending my stories to the same magazine, but the magazine wasn't buying.

My motivations for investing in the magazine weren't very subtle. I often think that the only story is the revenge story, and this was a kind of revenge. During my brief time working as a writer, a time marked by the disappearance of general interest magazines, the *New Yorker* had become *the* place to place a story.

My friends who were writers talked endlessly about the magazine. We computed our chances of publication: 52 weeks in a year, 2.5 stories per week if you count the funny ones. As an object of obsession the magazine seemed to be playing along, magnifying its mystery. It wasn't just a hard nut to crack. All magazines seemed to be. *Atlantic* and *Harper's* had their puzzles. The *New Yorker* itself was a puzzle that sucked me in—no masthead, no bio notes. I hate to admit it. The more rejections I got, the more remote the possibility of publishing there, the more I wanted to. Nothing emits exclusiveness like the *New Yorker*. You tell yourself that there isn't any one way to become a writer in America, no real certificate, no degree that really matters. But there is this dirty little secret, isn't there? The *New Yorker* might be the most prurient mag on the rack. You shouldn't want this but you do. You feel cruddy six or seven different ways.

When you're cynical, it's nice to have money. I bought some stock. And I felt better. Of course, what with the compartmentalizing of the magazine into the watertight departments of business and editorial, I wasn't really in. I did get the accountant's rush of counting. I was the bottom line. I had a kind of inside track. It was my magazine now. I knew how things really worked.

The dividend checks were cute with the funny guy looking at the butterfly, the winking owl perched on the $ sign. The annual report was written in the same style as "The Talk of the Town." The years I held the stock, the place was losing money, not a lot, but the trend was clear. Sure, it lessened the sting of those rejections I was still receiving. I luxuriated in my fiduciary knowledge. I knew about the job security, the health plans, the retirement benefits of the anonymous editors and readers who returned my stories. I felt the tiny power of that knowledge and weighed it against the little scrap of paper, and, I guess, I felt revenge. But it was pretty pitiful. I still was stuck with my own personal problems of desiring the wrong things and not being grateful for the things I did have.

I made a lot of money when the *New Yorker* was bought out. I made more money then than I have ever made writing fiction. But even ironically this story isn't satisfying. Yes, that's right. The money meant very little; the revenge wasn't sweet. I tell you this story not to make a point about values but to suggest how profound and subtle are the connections between those who write and those who publish what is written.

I suspect that in a collection of essays about contemporary writing little time will be spent musing on the material sources of what's being published. The *New Yorker* does play a role in all of this. But what? The mass hysterias of the age may be created by God but are just as likely caused by a mold secreting hallucinogenic enzymes in rye flour.

If there is an "Iowa" poem, then there is a *New Yorker* story. My purpose is not to try to define what that *New Yorker* story is but simply to remind everyone that we often proceed as if that definition is widely understood. Saying so makes it so. Only in my darkest moments do I inflate the editors of the magazine to the level of conspirators, inside traders, manipulators of the story market. My own feeling is that the magazine's real influence reaches beyond what it chooses to include as fiction. The magazine's real power over fiction is in the way it approaches fact. It elevates the real. It stands for accuracy. Its message finally is that of the last word.

What I am trying to get at is the catalytic effect of such an agent in the world of fiction. In the presence of such overwhelming fact, fiction is transformed. Jay McInerney, in his book *Bright Lights, Big City*, brings this notion full circle. He nominates a member of the famous fact-checking department as the Jake Barnes of the current lost generation. McInerney himself is infected by the same attention to detail he details. His narrator scrupulously informs the reader of the exact name of this or that bar. In the middle of a poignant moment, as the main character sits with his dying mother, McInerney carefully annotates the venue of the visit, Manchester, with New Hampshire so there will be no mistake.

McInerney portrays the fact checkers somewhere between Disney dwarfs and the three Fates of Greek mythology. But I like to think of their real-life counterparts more as the Federal Reserve Board, regulating the various supplies of reality, inflating the literal to literature. What power the magazine and its fact checkers possess multiplies in direct proportion to the extent they remain mysterious. That is, the less you know about the *New Yorker*, the more mythic it becomes, the more powerful is its vision of reality. That vision of reality becomes real. Voodoo economics.

What does this climate do for fiction writers? We are importing visionaries from South America along with hamburger patties, great-looking shoes, and tropical fruit. I wonder as I write my own stories what stays my hand, what keeps me down to earth. Both Joe David Bellamy in his introduction to the anthology *Superfiction* and Tobias Wolff in his forward to *Matters of Life and Death* begin with abdications to the factual world. As Philip Roth suggests in his essay "Writing American Fiction," who wouldn't have given teeth to have created Richard Nixon? In the U.S., the world has always been too much with us. One way or another our stories are contorted by the perceived efficacy and efficiency of the factual world. I am convinced that the *New Yorker* plays a role in converting the smoke of fiction into the scrubbed exhaust of fact. It is, at least, rendered harmless, breathable. The magazine is a kind of machine in the garden, transforming the New World into New Jersey.

I took the money I made when Newhouse bought out the magazine and put it all into a toy company called Ohio Art. It's traded on the American exchange. The company's major product is the Etch A Sketch. They still make thousands of those thin red plastic boxes with that magic silver screen. You remember. You twisted the knobs, one for the vertical and one for the horizontal, and a picture appeared on the screen. When you turned the thing over and shook it, the screen magically re-silvered. If you were like me, you patiently nudged the etched line up and down, back and forth, trying to scratch off all of that metallic powder to see into the guts of the device, to find out how it worked. It was hours and hours of fun.

pace Dome

As the end of the century approached, I found myself teaching at Syracuse University. The editors of the university's magazine asked me, a fiction writer, to speculate on the future of the campus. I focused my thoughts on the massive Carrier Dome right outside my window, the most futuristic-looking building in the Gothic landscape. Syracuse in the early nineties had just been wired to the Web. The memos from now on would be electronic.

Where are you when you are on hold? And when you finally get through to that 800 operator, where do the two of you meet? I always ask now when I do get through to order from a catalog or make a reservation. Where are you? The answer comes back. Omaha, say, or Rapid City, or some fringe city outside Atlanta. But, we know, we are meeting somewhere else, at a crossroads that is becoming quite familiar to us all.

You catch yourself there as you navigate the ever-branching logic trees of your ATM or as you channel surf along coaxial cable or on the beam emanating from a geosynchronous satellite. I'm there now as I type this onto the excitable phosphorescent screen of my computer. Oh sure, we leave the husks of our bodies behind us in the lobby of the bank, in the reclining lounger, in the swivel chair tucked next to this desk, but more and more we all have experienced the sensation of this placelessness where the thinking part of us takes part in what seems like some vast architecture of a much larger overarching mind.

It used to be we talked of the ghost in the machine. These new machines make us conscious of the ghosts within us. We sense those ghosts leaving us, leaving our corporeal selves, sparking across the synapses between our fingertips and keypads. Or they depart by way of the breathy current of our voices as our bodies linger in cruise-controlled autos, drifting from cell to cell, along those now old, now not-so-super super highways. Cyberspace, the novelist William Gibson has dubbed this place, the rooms of virtual reality with its ether of data, its plasma of text, its atmosphere of simulation. Cyberspace is getting to feel like home. Hold has got a hold on us.

Syracuse University has initiated the "Commitment for Learning" campaign with the goal of raising $300 million by the turn of the century, and this effort has been coupled with a fair amount of speculation about the shape of the university's future and the shape of the university itself in that future. *Syracuse Magazine* has asked me to imagine the university in the new millennium.

I teach creative writing at the university here and now, and I suspect the editors of this publication envisioned a creative response. Might I cast a landscape akin to the fantasy illustrations of the popular science magazines of my youth, a tomorrow filled with gyrocopters, pneumatic tubing, meals condensed into pills, and the sweeping panoramic vision of a great crystalline domed city. Such musing would provide an antidote, perhaps, to the cut-and-dried development story announcing the fund-raising effort and the practical goals of its funding. But, as science fiction writers are fond of saying, the future ain't what it used to be.

Alas, my imaginative prowess doesn't run along the Jules Vernesque line. I'm not so much a Luddite as locked in this time. I tend in my own storytelling to cast tales set in the place where I'm from, Planet Indiana I'm calling it, firmly rooted in, what I called before, the here and now. And it is true, official versions of the university's future are short on the gee-whiz, Buck Rogers kind of creativity. Besides, my taste in the future tends to be apocalyptical in its expression, the anti-utopia of *Blade Runner,* where the nifty video pay phones of tomorrow still are scrawled all over with graffiti. In the university's vision, there is no nostalgia for the future but sober projections from statistical foundations.

Electronic classrooms are projected, of course, crammed with the hard-wired accoutrements of the interactive future, computers with scads of memory modemed to webs and wells, everything one needs in a tastefully appointed node on the net.

As I suggest above, this is no giant leap for us to make. Images of such a future are as accessible to us now as the most recent telephone commercial. Imagine, its talking head prompts, a classroom in the boonies, in Indiana let's say, plugged into the lecture of the foremost authority of this or that.

I think we think that Syracuse University classrooms of the future, so wired and equipped, will be the platforms from which such lectures are launched or will be the landing pads for incoming global expertise. But there is a question to be begged in such a possibility. This projected future assumes that a place like a classroom, the physical space where we now gather, need exist at all. It is perhaps that gloomy apocalyptic nature of mine that makes me wonder.

In the Cyberspace sketched out in my opening, I suggest we are already gathering without the benefit of much physical plant. All we need is voltage, some solid-state boxes, and the wire, though maybe not even the wire, to get on-line. In this future why would anyone actually transport to the actual Syracuse, to come to the space of these now ancient, and now getting older by the minute, classrooms?

Let's continue thinking about wire.

Syracuse is a lot like my hometown of Fort Wayne, Indiana. They have a similar population and ethnic mix. The cities grew along canals and railroads, have auto plants and electric companies in their histories. I live in a house built in the teens of this century at the same time and on the same plans as the one I grew up in, an old foursquare design. Daydreaming, I can easily drift back and forth between these places, mistake one for the other, even wake as a child, for a minute, in my old room.

I walk down Euclid to get to the university, and it is wire that I notice. The utility poles are bearing a bumper crop of cable, wrapped like vines coiling into huge spliced trunks. Nynex and the cable television companies have been stringing fiber-optic line, anticipating the synthesis of all our electronic machines — telephone, computer, television, fax — into one new machine. NiMo, the electric company, tends the stringy arbor by topping the overgrown oaks and maples to weave the insulated, high-tension kudzu through the branches.

When I moved to Syracuse this cable canopy registered in my mind as a distinguishing detail of this place. In Fort Wayne, a copy of Syracuse in so many ways, the residential blocks are cut with alleys, and the services are strung on poles behind the garages. Syracuse, for me, will always be the place where the old houses are screened by this grid of the grid.

How do we know where we are? Of course we notice certain things in our surroundings and store away these orientating details, creating a kind of cognitive map of the place. The urban planner Kevin Lynch, in his book *The Image of the City*, actually had residents of Boston, Jersey City, and Los Angles draw maps and narrate their daily journeys through their cities. Lynch paid attention to the references that overlapped, the landmarks most people steer by, and discovered whole regions of the cities that were invisible even to the inhabitants of those neighborhoods. He attempted to articulate principles of our recognition. He noticed, for instance, that Bostonians tended to draw the Charles River first, a solid boundary edge to their spatial knowledge, and that the citizens of that city liked to imagine their Boston, in their own minds, from across that river, a sweeping panorama in which they also imagined themselves enmeshed.

In all the talk of Syracuse University's future there is not much print spent on the physical feel of this place. The focus of this campaign is not to raise money or to raise new buildings. Lynch's work points out that the connections we make with our surroundings are stored deep in our memories, so deep, it seems, that the particulars approach a kind of invisibility. Our surroundings become a steady state of sensual bombardment, and we, as the old song says, don't know what we've got 'til it's gone.

The university, we know, will be student-centered, but where will the student be centered? Remember that the revolution in electronic media, also spelled out in our future, may render the idea of going any *place* obsolete. So why come to Syracuse? What is the *where* here? Where is the *here* here?

I'd like to nominate the idea of the Dome to answer those questions. That is, I like it as an idea, a metaphor perhaps, that represents this place and its future.

Let's begin with basics. Because it is an unsupported roof, the pressurized atmosphere propping up the ceiling, there is a simple elegance to its implication. The Dome defines an open space while at the same time that open space defines the Dome.

To be in the Dome when it is empty of other people is to catch a fleeting sensation of space itself. The scale of the Dome is large enough to suggest your true size in relationship to the greater sphere outside the Dome, and yet the limits of this dome are perceptible. The translucent billow of the ceiling appears, simultaneously, invisible and sheltering. It is architecture expressed simply, a space defined by a single element—one circular wall that arches overhead everywhere—and its very simplicity suggests the profound complexity of the notion of "space" and of our relationships to it—outside and inside, here and there, small and large.

Of course, the Dome, on less abstract terms, encapsulates this university. Filled to capacity with the fans of football games or commencement exercises it defines the community by containing so many of its members at one time. Little wonder that this space within the larger space of the campus registers on the cognitive maps of its inhabitants. Everyone, sooner or later, dances across its ceremonial floor in the strange ritual garb of tuxedos, plaid field-hockey skirts, academic robes, or band busbies.

The Dome serves as an orienting landmark in our minds as it also serves as the actual site of orientation for the prospective students who graze the gridiron on campus tours or the matriculating freshmen who take their bearings on arrival. This is the place. This is the hive into which you have entered. This is the concave lens that magnifies your own daily efforts, blends them into a focal point with the ordinary diverse energy being generated from the busy mass of people all around you.

That's the inside. Outside, the Dome, as a building, always seems to brood behind the university's skyline, to hover just out of reach. Its roof floats like the balloon it is, caught fleetingly it seems, wedged between the sharp vertical edges of the university's other buildings. Standing in the quad, your gaze can take in all of Hendricks Chapel with its silver dome or the entire edifice of the old Carnegie Library with its domed cupolas. But behind each perspective is only a fragment of the Dome, levitating like a cartoon thought bubble above our heads.

On campus the Dome is always in the periphery. Which is to say that, though it is always on the edges of our seeing it and, thus, unseen, it is still always there.

Architects like Kevin Lynch would say that the Dome has no feet because it towers above us, which is how we know it. Its base is unimagined, forgotten, lost, and, indeed, I am always surprised when I drive down the little ramp past the law school and hurtle up against the ribbed wall. I think, It is this close after all.

The other day, the quilting of the Dome's roof draped above Archbold gym made me think of the foremost tops and flying gallants of the old tall ships, their metropolis of sails. Or, as my gaze fell back down to earth, I thought, yes, that slice of the roof could be the rounded back of a sounding whale. Look, the reinforcing ribs and lightning vanes could be the debris of harpoons and lines scoring the flanks of the Great White Whale. Melville mused on the whiteness of that whale. Here the Dome takes on the role of transubstantiation. The whiteness of the Dome. A cloud. A snow-drift. Mushroom. The moon rising in our midst. A fissured skull. Trampoline. Marshmallow. Down comforter. The Dome is an eerie presence, attractive and unknowable, hidden and dominating. It functions as the blank projection screen of our daydreams, its otherworldliness a locus for our imagination. The thing itself could be an icon for the brain.

From the elevated highways running through the city, the whole sweeping curve of the Dome can be seen as a kind of shell scalloped behind the towers of the Hall of Languages and Crouse College. Or you can see it another way. The Dome isn't fanned out behind the skyline like a screen. The Dome's outline is really tracing another dome, much bigger and transparent, that now seems to enclose the whole campus.

It turns out then that my vision of this place *has* included one of those old time science-fiction vistas, the domed city on the hill, which encompasses both the founding Methodists' own visions of the future and those from the pulp fiction of the 1950s.

The campus is pleasant to look at from any angle. The hill it rests on is itself dome-shaped, and the Dome upon it mirrors the surrounding ring of domed drumlins draped in their smoky clouds of leafless trees. Every picture of the campus must be composed around the Dome, its centerpiece, its pinnacle, our own unmelted snow-capped cap.

Wherever he moves, David Hamilton, a professor at the University of Iowa, notices that residents of a place ask an indigenous question. When he was in Charlottesville, he told me, the question was, *what church will you be attending?* When he moved to the University of Michigan, people asked, *what work do you do?* And when he moved to Iowa, he was asked, *what do you garden?* Syracuse's indigenous question must have to do with the weather, with winter specifically. In practical and functional terms, the Dome's construction was a response to the climate, perhaps more that than anything else. It is a complicated answer to our own indigenous question.

In lighter moments, as I am rushing along 690, I imagine that domed campus on the hill I see in the distance as one of those souvenir snow globes. I place a Plexiglas bubble over it all, with those lake effect flakes that seem to appear spontaneously out of the liquid air around us, a localized blizzard. Our igloo. That's how it feels here in Syracuse, doesn't it? The roofs we throw up over us are roofed themselves by something larger, this particular dome of saturated sky, this unique vault of frescoed clouds.

The space I have been writing about is not Cyberspace. It is the old-fashioned kind, cobbled out of old physical material, bricks and mortar, and their high-tech yet humble descendents—steel and nylon, concrete and plastic. Once such old-fashioned space was new. The Romans, when they built the first dome, thought they had defined space itself, meta-space, in a building. The Pantheon, they hoped, contained all of heaven under its dome, or, probably closer to the truth, contained the desire to contain all of heaven.

People have been fashioning new spaces forever. The most recent expansive configuration is now expressed in the paradox of miniaturization that has given us this seemingly infinite accordion sensation of space. There are rooms within rooms within rooms within rooms in Cyberspace. And it is interesting, in passing, to note that this new space uses the old metaphors of rooms and roads to help us navigate within it and through it.

Of course, in all of this space, it is the orchestration of meeting that becomes important.

Keep that orchestration in mind. You will better understand the seemingly modest goals the university has of identifying certain creative combinations of teacher and learner, its objectives of finding a particular kind of student, and its desires to sustain such contact through an array of financial and material support. It assumes without question (I have brought the question up here) the inherent value of face-to-face meetings and does so in the face of new technologies that make other inter-faces readily possible.

The happy babbling heads we meet as artfully arranged pixels on our television screens keep telling us, when we receive them in the cocoon of our wired homes, that the only space that matters is the expanse beneath the domes of our skulls. That's where the action is. Reality, virtual or not, takes place there in the gelatinous matter between our ears. The question at hand, so to speak, is *where is the mind?* The boosters of a cybernetic future are rooting for the brain alone. They might be right. Let's say they are right. Then even before all the newfangled hardware, we were already walled up in the bounded precincts of our own consciousness. Universities have always been about the demolition of those walls and the creation of a space hospitable to a variety of experience. You can think of the university as a machine as well, a huge one, one that resists reinforcing the solipsistic tendencies wired into us, while it amplifies the social ones. The university is a space that makes room for minds to meet and defines the mind as that dialectic bundle of brain and body.

Kevin Lynch in his books about the notion of place suggests why students in the future will continue to come to places like Syracuse. A place, he points out, emerges within a component of time that is shared by a cohort of contemporaries. There are bands of graduates roaming the earth now whose sense of Syracuse is a shared reference point in time. To some it might be the wire-lined streets of the neighborhood before the dorms were built. To others it could be the little amphitheater of heather and limestone commemorating the victims of Pan Am flight 103. To both groups the sense of "Syracuse" will be vastly different, but for both, "Syracuse" will be created from their particular time here. For others it might be the brick lobby of Schine, the steps of Hendricks Chapel, a booth at the Varsity, a table on the ground floor of Bird, or even the computer cluster in HBC. The intersection of lives leaves a residue in this nonvirtual reality, in this reality. Evidence of such shared experience is erased in Cyberspace, is, by definition, Cyberspace. Nothing and no one is left to mark the shared passage.

Take the Observatory, another dome. It is one of those landmarks that mark a place in time. To some graduates it figures as a classroom, to others a ruin. The building has even been moved like a castle on a chessboard so that some alumni cognitive maps need replotting. Ironic, no? A building built to fix time and space itself involved in moving, literally and metaphorically, in time and space. Today the Observatory is home to the Soling project, perhaps a working model for the university's future, groups of students and professors rearranging the space of the classroom through collaborative and community work. I went to look under the old dome of that building. The telescope is long gone, its efficacy washed out by the city's lights. Its one big room now hosts teams of students and faculty who report to each other their interdisciplinary journeys out into the world. It is as if the building's original purpose has been turned inside out. The observation now encompasses both inner and outer space, and the lenses have been trained on the city lights below the hill. Here is a new nexus being built where a community is making a time and place.

I have dwelt on the Dome for what it might symbolize as well as what it is. A dome by definition is a covered space with no obstructing support. Our Dome is that sheltered egalitarian arena where all of us and all of each of us can dance our dance. I am attracted to the bulk of the real Dome, to its physical presence and to its airy emptiness. It seems at once ancient and futuristic. It makes me think of space and how space metamorphoses into place. This place, Syracuse, where I find myself right now, while staring at a screen into my future, is still attached to this old, old architecture of flesh and bone.

# Four Factual Anecdotes on Fiction

In 2002 Paul Maliszewski edited *McSweeney's* number 8 and included this essay in the mix along with some of my fiction and a fictional contributor's note.

1.   At the end of the Second World War, my grandfather responded to a radio appeal broadcast by General Mark Clark, who was governing occupied Austria, for Americans to send packages of food and other vital necessities to the refugees, displaced persons, and homeless civilians of a devastated Europe. That very day my grandfather sent his first care package. He told me, years later, that he tried to imagine what a family in circumstances he could not imagine would want or need. He sent potted meat, paper and pencils, chocolate bars and gum, evaporated milk, a pack of playing cards, a can opener, flour and sugar, envelopes, needles and thread and buttons and zippers, coffee and tea. He also sent peanut butter.

His monthly charity was assigned to a family in Vienna, the Gabauers, who wrote back using the equipment my grandfather had supplied, thanking him and meticulously inventorying the contents of each subsequent package. I have read the letters. The exchange of goods and the receipt of letters went on for three years after the end of the war. The Gabauers were initially confused by the peanut butter. "What is 'peanut butter'?" At first they used it as cooking oil and then as leavening in their baking. The letters, in German, had been translated by a friend of my grandfather, the English penciled in between the lines of German, a layered sandwich of languages. Eventually the family figured out what to do with the peanut butter, but they also wrote—a daughter usually wrote—of their evolving life in recovering Austria, their growing but meager prosperity. They sent detailed renderings of local color and narratives about their attempts to learn English. There are eighty-three letters, most written on the paper my grandfather sent. I have them still, having inherited them when my grandfather died.

I used the above anecdote in a story once, changing a few of its details to make it, well, fiction, of course, and a better story. I elaborated on other details and added new ones. In the story, the narrator, a young man, a college student, is encouraged by his grandfather to learn German in school. Once the young man learns the language, his grandfather reveals that he had sent care packages to a family in Austria after the war. They, in turn, had sent letters to the grandfather, who can now, years after their composition and with the help of his educated grandson, translate their thanks, their daily observations, their confusion about peanut butter. The letters, in my story, had lain dormant for thirty years awaiting the fictional scene in which a character very much like me reads them in order of reception for the first time to his grandfather. The final letters, when translated, wonder why the grandfather has never written back. The family begs him to stop sending packages, indicates they are back on their feet. In fact, the daughter who has now learned the language writes the very last letter, in my story, in English. That letter, the one in English, has not been opened until the present time of the story, thirty years after its initial writing, at the end of the story.

I wrote the story not long before my grandfather died. I read it to him. The story ends with a scene where the grandson is reading a letter to the grandfather in the kitchen of the grandfather's apartment that was very much like the one where I sat reading my grandfather the story. He said, as I finished, using my diminutive pet name to address me, that, yes, I had got it exactly right, that the story was exactly as he remembered it.

How curious, I thought. I was quite conscious that the story I had written and had just then read, with its made-up particulars and invented circumstance, had at that very moment overwritten the actual memory in my grandfather's mind. It was as if my dream of the story had infected my grandfather's dreaming of his own life. I had never learned German. He had given me the letters a long time ago to read and admire. I had known since high school the story of the Gabauers, of reading the mortar of English between the blocks of solid German. "You got that right, Mickey," he said.

I didn't say anything to dissuade him of his belief. He was, I could see, delighted to remember these events of his life. Perhaps he was simply delighted to remember any events of any life. In a few months he would be dead and all his memories erased. In the meantime he avidly told any of the other residents of his building who cared to listen the story, recently, from his point of view, recalled. There was the war, Mark Clark, the packages, the Gabauers, their letters only now translated by his grandson, and the sad and funny search found within them for the uses of peanut butter.

2a. The Gideons usually work in pairs, holding down a strategic corner or crosswalk at the gateways of the campus. They show up twice a year. Boxes of the little green, gold-trimmed Bibles are at their feet. They dip into the boxes, scooping out a handful of books. They hand the books to the students as they shuffle past. I have a collection of these Gideon Bibles. Twenty-five years of Bibles. They are all exactly the same. The leather-like wrapper, the pocket size, the prohibition against selling this book. Many students, as they put some distance between themselves and the Gideons, seek to dispose of their gifts. I always like it when the result is the spontaneous decoration of a nearby shrub or bush, the Bibles trimming the branches, scattered like presents on the carpet of needles beneath the lowest limbs. The Gideons never seem to pick up the discards as they depart. Theirs is a mission of mine laying. It is the distribution that matters. One day the little package will find its mark, or more exactly the mark will stumble upon it by accident at a vulnerable moment. The Bible as crisis intervention, an 800 number on a refrigerator magnet. The opening pages gloss the content. Labeled "Where to Find Help When," this directory is followed by a list of afflictions and the corresponding verse. Where to Find Help When—Afraid, Anxious, Backsliding, Bereaved, Bitter, etc. Boom, boom, boom. I am reminded of the entomologist who imported the gypsy moth parasite and released it into the infestation and nothing happened. He went to his grave thinking his efforts had been a failure when only recently, after years and generations, the parasite has just now reached a critical population mass and has begun to do its work.

2b.   Also appearing seasonally on campuses are itinerant preachers who in the middle of the quad or yard accost the students, pestering, proselytizing. The strategy is to get the students to stop. You do that through accusation, condemnation. You want them to heckle, argue, and hence attract a crowd. Once I wrote a play about an itinerant preacher who comes to a college campus and, using the above techniques, engages students as they mill about the campus. I didn't know much more of what would happen or how it was going to end. It was to be performed on the quad with only a few actors who would perform the roles of the preacher and students; the rest of the play would proceed improvisationally through audience participation of real students thinking that they were witnessing an ordinary appearance of an actual itinerant preacher. There would be in this audience, the one innocent of the fiction of the performance, another audience, this one in on the fiction. That was several semesters ago. Every year since, in the fall and the spring when the weather is fine and the preachers appear, I go out to watch the performance. I even participate, calling out some lines I have composed for the occasion. I never know now what I am watching. I have to, finally, make up my mind about what I am seeing. Am I watching my play or is it a play written by someone else? Sooner or later, I go ahead and see it one way or the other, an illusion I switch back and forth in my head.

3.   I went to a circus. It was an old-fashioned circus, one ring and wood bleachers in a battered canvas tent set up in a city park. The members of the circus company all did many jobs. The ringmaster sold tickets. The lady on the trapeze, when she finished her act, came back down to earth and sold popcorn in the stands. Clowns came out between the tumbling or wire acts to distract the audience while the trampolinist-turned-roustabout rerigged the ring. The only animal act, appropriate to the scale, was a dog one. The dogs, dressed in dog tuxedoes, walked around on their hind legs. So one of the intervening clown acts made fun of the circus's lowered expectations. This clown act was a parody of an equestrian performance. There was one horse and its trainer. The horse was a two-piece affair, head and tail sections, a burlap getup. The clown trainer wore the red riding tails and top hat and repeatedly injured himself with his own whip. The horse did a lot of business in which the front and tail end disagreed. The front end was the straight man, naturally, its legs crossed casually as the unruly ass end danced around behind. The clunky head would snap around to stare down the revolting rear half which, when spied, would freeze and act nonchalant, shuffling its droopy hooves casually. The clown played to both ends, appealing to each to perform the tricks he was eliciting. I was thoroughly convinced that I was watching men dressed up like a horse. The disguised pair were talented enough to, at moments, make me believe I was seeing, even though the costume was so shabby, a real horse. And at that moment they would do something to remind me, lift the fake tail, say, that I was really watching an elaborate, full-sized puppet. I am allergic to real horses, and suddenly I felt allergic as I watched this performance. I remember thinking, This is marvelous, the illusion so convincing at times that I am behaving as if I were in the presence of the actual animal. Even as I began to sneeze, I thought it must be a reaction to the burlap or the hay the horse refused to eat.

The interlude drew to a close, and the clown trainer took his bow. The horse, too, awkwardly genuflected its front legs, bowing while tossing its hollow head. The clown moved toward the seam in the fabric at the horse's waist. He tugged at the burlap and the disguise fell away, revealing not the team of operating clowns, but another horse. But this horse was not a costume of a horse. It was a real horse that had just finished performing a counterfeit of men who are dressed up like a horse. My immune system, the one making me sneeze, had not been fooled, but every other sensing system, all of them completely shorted out by this revelation, were now taking a very pleasant second or two to come back on-line.

4.   A woman I know wrote her dissertation in geography on places in the world that had become real once they had been read about in a story. These places were now destinations for tourists: Green Gables, The House of Seven Gables, Sunnybrook Farm. People went to see the fence Tom Sawyer painted, walk the street Ishmael walked on his way to the sea. The insurance company occupying the offices of Sherlock Holmes assigns an employee to answer the detective's mail. In the Mediterranean there are tours that follow the course of the *Odyssey*. In Dublin there are organized odysseys as well. I published sections of *The Blue Guide to Indiana* in weekly newspapers in southern Indiana. They were presented without any indication of their fictional nature as places to see and things to do in Indiana. I did this for several reasons. I liked the idea of a fiction without character or plot, a fiction that provides instead costumes and props for the reader to employ. It is, after all, a tour guide. The fiction then is a collection of stuff, residue, evidence. Another woman I know wrote her dissertation on the use of labels in museums. She was all for them. It turns out to be a big debate in museum school, labels. I'm all for museums without labels, a museum where the clientele is let loose with artifacts to make heads or tails of the junk on their own. I like the idea of someone coming upon this fiction, not knowing it is even fiction, and having to ask, what is this? We all are constantly sifting through the detritus of the world trying to make a sense of it.

One day I got a call from a reporter from the *Washington Post*. He told me he was doing a story on little-known federal facilities and programs. I knew what he was about to ask. I had published a tour from *The Blue Guide* in a little newspaper. The tour concerned sites having to do with death: The Tomb of Orville Redenbacher, The Cemetery at Naked City, The National Monument for Those Killed by Tornadoes in Trailer Parks and Mobile Home Courts. There was also the Federal Research and Testing Center for Coffin and Casket Standards. The reporter was interested in the testing facility. Did I know anything about that? He had been led to believe I might know something about it. I thought about maintaining the illusion or at least remaining deadpan. But I told him I had made it up.

"I made it up," I said.

"Oh," he said, "that's too bad. This was one of the more interesting ones. I wanted this one to be for real."

ount Rushmore

FOUR BRIEF ESSAYS ON FICTIONS

I contributed these essays to *Symplokē* magazine. They are part of a larger book I have been working on for years called *Four for a Quarter*, a collection of stories and essays dependent on the number four — four corners of the world, four chambers of the heart, four winds, 4-H, foursquare, the four questions, etc.

Washington

Freud fucked us up, this Father business. The Mother business as well. He, Sigmund, is the inventor of the modern novel, is *the* novelist of the twentieth century, the founder of the form. He is the Father — that again — of the notion of Character and even more importantly the notion of the character of Character, this business of depth, this business of three dimensions, this business of complex. The forefather of the epiphany of The Epiphany and the transformation of transformation of Character that follows. He, Freud, elicits in me a kind of envy, yes, Envy, that I have not, in all my years, invented or, in all my years to come, will never invent, any Character as real as Ego, as real as Id. There! There are fictions for you, so contagious as to jump the page, reformulate the brain chemistry so completely as to deny the efficacy and accuracy of Brain Chemistry to explain the brain. His invention of the Subconscious, the Unconscious naturalizes inside us (Inside

Us!) the idea of the Subconscious, the Unconscious (See!) as if these fictions are not fictions. I like the bib of slag spilling down the General's chest, a graphic demonstration that the head of the Head of State was always in state there inside the mountain. See the limestone-wigged helmet of the figurehead on the brow of the cliff ship! The lithic waste is the cascading, foaming bow wake. George is a kind of Venus in drag and Penis in person, the titanic member being the progenitor of his Country, sure, but also Love, I guess, or at least that compelling drive of Sex, emerging from the sea of solid rock.

Jefferson

He was the writer. Well, Lincoln, too, wrote, signed on to write Jefferson's sequel. And Jefferson is the one whose back-story has legs. The heritage of his transmitted DNA is decoded as avidly as the Declaration is parsed for intention. My favorite plot twist? The branch of Hemmings's children by Tom who passed into Ohio, refusing to cotton up to the analysis of their genes, preferring White-ness over Jefferson-ness. How odd our desire that this one have a life that is narrative, not simply anecdote. And irony too. Back-story, and there on the escarpment he's got George's back. The inventor of political parties, the originator of difference. The Great Deconstructor has the least "face." No distinguishing marks save that distinction of no distinguishing marks. Okay, red hair, but this is a monochromatic mountain. Jefferson pulls duty in two dimensions, flat visage on the screwy two-dollar bill. J is our K of presidents. Anonymous and somewhat known with the suggestion there are things one wants to know. And inside Jefferson is Madison, the symbiote inside the big brain, the watch in the pocket. Madison writes Jefferson; Jefferson writes *America*. *America* is the Great American Novel.

Roosevelt

Reading left to right: Roosevelt. The modernist whose medium is stuff, stuff like mountains, like canals, like painting battleships white and sending them on a performance piece around the world. Probably his idea to create the thing itself, this wacky stunt in South Dakota. Or at least it was in the air he breathed, expelled. His is the spitting image of the contemporaneous zeitgeist; the modesty of the placement of his visage tips off the self-consciousness of the facade. The least equal of these equal giants but nonetheless the Great Sculptor of the ideal of giants. The last of firsts but the first of lasts. There is real artistry in the rendering of the pince-nez. The glasses are there but not. A transparent reproduction of Transparency. Transparency the dominant ideology of the age, our age. The trick of realism, its tricklessness. See, these busts bloomed on the mountaintop, a spontaneous generation like maggots appearing on rotting meat. WYSIWYG is what you see and what you get from this point on. No bull. The eye is drawn to those eyes, magnified by the invisible glass. What are you looking at? The writing of novels, I think, is so beside the point, isn't it? One writes novels to write the author of the novel. The book itself does not last, is not carved on the side of a mountain, is not printed on money. Funny, the New Critical transparency was to focus on The Work and not The Author of The Work. But it is always Marvell's "To His Coy Mistress." Every work comes with that apostrophe of possession. The Author ain't dead. The Author ain't even ain't.

Lincoln

The most dead one. How did Washington die? Jefferson? Roosevelt? Lincoln's death was the one dramatized, in a theater no less, by an actor acting and acting. History is scripted. The show goes on. Literally, the show goes on. *Our American Cousin* performed daily like clockwork. The clocks all set for ten after ten. Whatever happened to pageants? The great theatrical recreations of historical events by ordinary citizens, descendants of the participants in the original events, on the sites where the original events first transpired? Sure, the Mormons perform each summer, on another mountain in New York, the visitation of the angel to the Prophet Joseph Smith. Now there's a novel! But the art form of the pageant, the pre-postmodern art form, seems to have waned. Perhaps. Perhaps pageantry continues but is only now disguised as Real Life, Story and History the same. The recent War in Iraq was staged. It was held in theater. How did the President watch the performance? Not that much differently than I did, I bet. Like a King in Shakespeare watching a play on stage upon the stage. Like the Subjects of a King watching the pageantry of royalty, of war. My favorite part was the soldier, wounded in the hand, waiting for the evacuation by helicopter, who had the word HAND written on his forehead, talking to his mother, a half a world away by satellite phone, talking to his mother in real time (Real Time!) while I watched. That was my favorite part. Lincoln's forehead was a stage. In the movie, *North by Northwest*. All of the presidents look on when the actor Cary Grant, playing the role of Roger Thornhill playing the role of Mr. Kaplan, performs a staged performance of his (Cary Grant playing Roger Thornhill playing Mr. Kaplan) death, all witnessed by the back-projected image of the mountain, there through the window by the barbershop quartet of stone. At the moment of the assassination The Real World approaches harmony with the Fiction of the World. *Sic Semper Tyrannis!*

Trying
AN INTRODUCTION[1] TO INTRODUCTION[2]
Four Found[3] Introductions[4]

I am a contributing editor to the *Colorado Review*. In 2001 David Milofsky, then the editor of the magazine, asked me to put together a special edition of experimental fiction. He also asked me to write a brief introduction. This is it. The title of the resulting anthology was *Trying Fiction*.

1. A. G. Bell hoped that "Ahoyahoy!" would be adopted. T. A. Edison pro-moted "Hello!" and he, as we now know, won out.

2. I am unaware of the introduction of the footnote in the history of print-ing. I suspect, however, the recent resurgence in its use in fiction has resulted from the push-button ease various software provide. Twenty some years into the P.C. era and writers are just now realizing they have been using their incredible typesetting and graphic-producing machines as typewriters. I am reminded of the years it took our civilization, once the physical labor of grain harvesting had been mechanized, to combine the individual procedures into one machine. Grain had been cut, bound, and threshed by hand. Individual machines were invented to cut, bind, and thresh. The "combine" was introduced a half century later.

3. More and more I tend to think of writing fiction as arranging found texts instead of composing my own. So the machine innovation that should actually be celebrated here is the television remote control, a superlative narrative delivery device.

4. I've just been working on a book of my own fiction called *Four for a Quarter*. So the selection of four as an organizing factor is highly arbitrary yet necessary once one abandons the narrative line in prose.

1. Introductions to Introductions[5]

I.[6]

The inferior should always be introduced to the superior—ladies take precedence of gentlemen; you will present the gentleman to the lady, not the lady to the gentleman.

II.

If on paying a morning visit you meet strangers at the house of your friend and are introduced, it is a mere matter of form, and does not entitle you to future recognition by such persons.

III.

Be very cautious of giving a gentleman a letter of introduction to a lady—it may be means of settling weal or woe of the persons for life.

IV.

If you wish to avoid the company of a gentleman who has been properly introduced, treat him with respect, at the same time shunning his company. But few will mistake you.[7]

2. Manner of the Introduction of Evidence during Trial[8]

5. From *True Politeness, Handbook of Etiquette for Ladies* by an American Lady, 1847.

6. I selected only four of sixteen rules listed under introductions. Again, my predilection for the number.

7. I just love the antique idiom here. It is like Victorian wallpaper. And, really, don't *try* to read anything into this. I just wanted to include it for its texture. Of course, there are certain startling effects when a piece of writing is taken out of context and reframed. A certain valence and strangeness, a strangeness for its own sake.

8. I had wanted to quote from the actual procedures recorded in Alabama's code, but I didn't get around to it. The law school here is way out on Paul W. "Bear" Bryant Drive. I could call my lawyer, Joseph Pierce, but I am, as it turns out, in the middle of suing somebody. It is a Dickensian tale having to do with a temporary fiction instructor I hired for the department and his moving company. Not enough time to explain, but the judgment I got here in Alabama needed to be

3. An Introduction to Lab Ware[9]

The origins of laboratory glassware reach back to vessels used by medieval alchemists, the cucurbits and alembics and retorts in which they tried to transmute lead into gold, and by doing so understand the ineffable intentions of God.[10]

4. Introduction[11]

The secret to writing a good[12] narrative:

"domesticated" in a court in Florida. I've been told by Joe that the "domestication" has been completed. How about that for some language? It has been two years now. I am suing for five thousand dollars on the deal. I have no notion of how much this suit is going to cost me. Plenty, probably. So I didn't want to call Joe and ask to use his law books for a scrap of prose. Honestly, I was afraid he would bill me hours for that on top of everything else. I will tell you one thing: I should have just not given the driver of the moving van my credit card. He was from Montreal and kept saying, "Michael, my friend," with that accent, you know? I can tell you that Alabama has the longest state constitution, and it contains the most amendments of any. I think it is approaching one thousand amendments now. But I can't be sure of this. I really don't want to call a lawyer to find out.

9. From *Martha Stewart Living*, May 2001, page 188.

10. I first met David Milofsky, the editor of *Colorado Review*, in 1981. We were officemates at Iowa State University. We've stayed in touch since then. Recently he invited me to do an "experimental fiction" issue, but I really don't like the term "experimental." I like to think of this kind of fiction as "formal." That is, this fiction foregrounds the variety of forms of prose first. Anyway, this kind of "experimental" stuff has been around as long as the non-"experimental" stuff. So the inclusion of this introduction of lab ware is a little joke on "experimental" as a term, you see.

11. From *How to Write an Exciting Short Story* by Study Buddy, 1980.

12. You will probably note that I really am not interested in the question of goodness in this issue. I realize as a guest editor, a gatekeeper du jour, I guess I am supposed to worry about the quality and pedigree of the contributions. But, to tell you the truth, it's not my lookout. I approach the enclosed with curiosity first of all. I know many writers who feel that in addition to being writers they also have to patrol standards of writing. Me? I'm not out on that patrol. I have no idea if what you are about to read (or what you are reading now, for that matter) is good or bad. I'll let you decide. I just know there is a lot of it. This must be the experimental part! I was pretty lucky to have a chance to post the work enclosed. Hey, it's a periodical anyhow. This will only be around for a quarter or so.

In simple terms, a narrative is a story. And like all good stories, it includes three basic elements:

Problem: Get your characters in a race.

Struggle: Get your characters to jump hurdles.

Solution: Get your characters across the finish line.

Experienced writers know the key to writing a good narrative begins with the ending. That's right—the ending. The writer usually develops a clever ending first. Then he works backward, introducing material and incidents that lead up to the clever ending. The ending, like the finish to a race, separates the winners from the losers.

Consider a few tips that could make your project a little easier:

1. Choose a subject that you are familiar with.[13]

2. Select a subject that really happened.

3. Choose a common human problem.

4.[14] Select an interesting character.

---

13. Of course if I were writing a story along these lines, you bet I'd use this court case I've got going. Now there's a finish line I'd like to cross. I might involve you, gentle reader. I know who you are now. I mean there is this subscription list. So don't be surprised if you receive, in the near future (I hope), a letter from me asking you all to contribute to my legal fund.

14. I really do like fours. I am worried now, at the end of this introduction, that once I send it off to Fort Collins my typography won't match up with the magazine's, and you won't get the joke here of the footnote "4" next to the regular "4." I hope it works out. But, really, this footnote button is a hoot. Rereading the above, I just want to footnote everything.

ake Nothing Happen

For an anthology called *The Story Behind the Story* editors Peter Turchi and Andrea Barrett asked twenty-six writers who have worked as teachers in Warren Wilson College's low-residency MFA program to contribute a story and a brief essay discussing the process that created the fiction. What follows are both the essay and the story I contributed. The story, "The Moon over Wapakoneta," was also published in the magazine *Crazyhorse*.

I write about Indiana. I consider myself a regionalist. "The Moon over Wapakoneta" is from a new book of short fiction called *Planet Indiana*. It is my attempt to remain true to my regional subject matter while combining it with a new, for me, genre. In this case, that would be science fiction. Science Fiction Regionalism, then, is where this contribution aspires to be catalogued.

My basic take on this particular hybrid fiction is that, in the future, Indiana will be pretty much the same as it is in the present. My Indiana is a pleasant, unexciting place where nothing significant happens and from which its natives hope to one day escape. I suspect that not much happens in Indiana in the future as well. It was the case when I was in high school that underage kids would go over to nearby Ohio border towns to drink 3.2 beer. I suppose that in the future this practice will continue but that the accoutrements of travel and navigation for even those short distances will be somewhat upgraded. Yes, the corn in the fields will be replaced by a crop of solar collectors. The basic poignancy, however, for a narrator, for me, of such a journey through those fields would remain consistent over time. Both in the present and future, the sense that one is in the middle of nowhere strikes the dominant chord. In the future version this might be accentuated by the possibility that the moon itself would be in the process of being settled, and that would amplify the backwater, provincial feeling of the original place. The future, and fiction that contemplates it, is often about change and the dynamic of change. I am able, given this setting, to speculate on the dynamic of stasis and static.

So what does happen? A kid in the future gets drunk, looks at the moon, and goes home. Same as it ever was. Thus my particular problem was animating this sparse movement. I hoped to do it with the language of this drunken monologue, as the words of the narrator are the only thing percolating on that particular night and in this particular fiction. Fortunately for me, Wapakoneta, Ohio, one of those border towns Hoosier youth visit, was the birthplace of Neil Armstrong, the first human on the moon. The setting sets up the moon as the focus of the narrator's howling for the evening. What form that howling would take presented itself to me as the classic Japanese haiku with a particular fondness for Basho's frog jumping into the pond and his drunk attempting to hug the moon's reflection in the same or similar body of water. Also, I had to find a way to play with time in the form of the story. Time, it seemed to me, is theme, subject, motif as much as place. Or, put another way, time is a kind of place, a locale. I decided to push the technique of repetition, repeating the words "moon," "Ohio," and "Wapakoneta" as many times as I could. I wished that the story would itself, through this incantation, set up a kind of gravitational field as well, mirroring the inescapable force of gravity present that night to this particular narrator. Though this is a monologue, the other players in the drama, for me, continued to be time and gravity and the equilibrium of those forces, now and in the future, to strongly attract and repel and thereby keep the narrator and the reader both in flight and perfectly still.

The Moon over Wapakoneta

1.

There is the moon, full, over Wapakoneta, Ohio. Everybody I know has a sister or a brother, a cousin or an uncle living up there now. The moon is studded green in splotches, spots where the new atmospheres have stuck, mold on a marble.

2.

I'm drunk. I'm always drunk. Sitting in the dust of a field outside Wapakoneta, Ohio, I look up at the moon. The moon, obscured for a moment by a passing flock of migratory satellites flowing south in a dense black stream, has a halo pasted behind it. That meant something once, didn't it?

3.

When the moon is like it is now, hanging over Ohio, I come over to Wapakoneta from Indiana, where I am from. I am legal in Ohio, and the near beer they can sell to minors is so near to the real thing it is the real thing. I told you I was drunk. The foam head of this beer glows white in the dull light like the white rubble of the moon bearing down from above. Over there, somewhere, is Indiana, a stone's throw away.

4.

Everybody I know has a brother or cousin or whoever on the moon, and I am using this pilsner for a telescope. Where is everybody? The old craters are percolating. They've been busy as bees up there. Every night a new green explosion, another detonation of air. This is where I make myself belch.

5.

The reflection of the moon over Wapakoneta sinks into each flat black solar panel of this field where I sit, a stone swallowed by a pond. In the fields, the collectors pivot slowly, tracking even the paler light of the moon across the black sky. There's this buzz. Cicada? Crickets? No. Voltage chirps, generated as the moon's weak light licks the sheets of glass.

6.

Let's power up my personal downlink. Where am I? —I ask by nudging the ergonomic toggle. Above me, but beneath the moon over Ohio, a satellite, then perhaps another, peels away from its flock to answer my call. Let's leave it on. More satellites will cock their heads above my head, triangulating till the cows come home. But soft, the first report is in. Ohio, the dots spell out, Wapakoneta.

7.

What part of the moon is the backwater part? Maybe there, that green expanse inches from the edge where they are doing battle with the airless void, generating atmosphere from some wrangling of biomass. Yeah, back there under the swirl of those new clouds, some kid after a hard day of—what?—making cheese, lies on his back and has a smoke, consuming a mole of precious oxygen. He looks up at the earth through the whiffs of cloud and smoke and imagines some Podunk place where the slack-jawed inhabitants can't begin to imagine being pioneers, being heroes. There it is, Ohio.

8.

A pod of jalopies takes off from the pad of Mr. Entertainer's parking lot and races back to Indiana where it's an hour earlier. The road is lined with Styrofoam crosses, white in the moonlight, and plastic flowers oxidized by the sunlight. *X* marks the spot where some hopped-up Hoosier goes airborne for a sec and then in a stupor remembers gravity and noses over into the ditch next to a field outside of Wapakoneta on the trailing edge of Ohio.

9.

They are launching their own satellites from the moon; a couple of dozen a day, the paper says. Cheap in the negative *G*'s. Gee. I look hard at the moon. I want to see the moons of the moon. The moon and its moons mooning me. In Ohio I pull my pants down and moon the moon and its moons mooning me back. And then I piss. I piss on the ground, my piss falling, falling to earth, falling to the earth lit up by the moon, my piss falling at the speed of light to the ground.

10.

I am on the move. I am moving. Drawn by the gravitational pull of Mr. Entertainer with its rings of neon, I am steering a course by the stars. Better check in. More of the little buzz bombs have taken up station above my head. Surprise! I am in Wapakoneta. I am in Wapakoneta, but I am moving. I am moving within the limits of Wapakoneta. I like to make all the numbers dance, the dots on the screen rearranging. X, Y, and Z, each axis scrolling, like snow in a snow dome. The solar panels in the field around me slowly track the moon as it moves through the night sky.

11.

Over there in Indiana, it's an hour earlier. Don't ask me why. You cross a road, State Line Road, and you step back in time. It can be done. Heading home, I get this gift, an extra hour to waste. But wait! I lost one someplace coming here. I shed it when I crossed the street, like sloughing skin. It must be somewhere, here at my feet. This pebble I nudge with my toe. Just what time is it? I consult my other wrist, where the watch burbles, all its dials spinning, glowing softly, little moon. The laser beam it emits ricochets off my belt buckle, noses up to find its own string of satellites, bouncing around a bit, kicking the can, homing for home, an atomic clock on a mountain top out west, to check in on each millisecond of the passing parade; then, in a blink, it finds its way back to me here, makes a little beep. Beep! Here's the report: Closing Time.

12.

Mr. Entertainer is not very entertaining. It's powering down before my eyes; each neon sign flickers, sputters in each dark window. The whole advertised universe collapses in on the extinguished constellation of letters. How the hell did that happen? I had my eye on things, and the moon over Wapakoneta hasn't moved as far as I can tell. The rubble of the bar is illuminated now by that soft, indifferent, dusty light diffused through the dust kicked up by the departed cars. The slabs of its walls fall into blue shadow; its edges then drift into a nebulous fuzz, a cloud floating just above the ground.

13.

What time is it on the moon? It's noon there now. It's noon on the moon. From the stoop of the extinct bar, I consider the moon's midday that lasts for days, lunch everlasting, amen. They must get drunk on the light. They must drink it up. They must have plenty to spare. The excess is spilling on me, pouring on me down here in Ohio, enough light for me, a heavenly body, to cast a shadow on the studded gravel galaxy of the empty parking lot, a kind of timepiece myself, the armature of an impromptu moon dial, the time ticking off as my celestial outline creeps from one cold stone to the next.

14.

Cars on the road are racing back to Indiana. I hear them dribbling the sound of their horns in front of them, leaking a smear of radio static in the exhaust. I am looking for my clunker. It's around here someplace. According to my uplink, I am still in Wapakoneta. A slow night for the satellites, they have been lining up to affirm that consensus; a baker's dozen have been cooking up coordinates. I punch a button on my car key releasing the ultrasonic hounds hot on the magnetic signature of my piece of shit. The nearby solar panels pivot toward me, sensing the valence of my reflection, hunger for the light I am emitting. Hark! Somewhere in the vast relative dark the yodel of a treed automobile. I must calculate the vectors for my approach.

15.

Later, in Indiana, which is now earlier, I will remember back to this time, this time that is happening now, as I navigate by means of sonic boom to the bleat of my Mother Ship supposedly fastened to the edge of some solar panel field out there somewhere in the dark. But the sound is reverberating, gone Doppler, bouncing off the copse of antennae to the right, the bank of blooming TV dishes to the left. The night air has become acoustic, dampening the reports. I am getting mixed signals, and it seems my car is moving around me. That may be the case. Perhaps I left it in autopilot. It's nosing toward home this very minute, sniffing the buried wire, or perhaps it's just playing games with me, its own guidance system on some feedback loop, as it orbits under the influence of an ancient cruising pattern programmed long ago for the high-school drag in Fort Wayne. My guardian satellites, whispering to each other, hover above my head, shaking theirs, "Lost, poor soul, in Ohio, in the holy city of Wapakoneta."

16.

Everybody I know has a sister or a brother, a mom or a dad setting up housekeeping in some low-rent crater of the moon. I intercept postcards—low-gain transmissions of the half earth in the black sky and a digital tweet eeping "Wish you were here!"—when I eavesdrop on the neighborhood's mail. On nights like this, with the moon radiating a whole spectrum of sunny missives, I want to broadcast a wideband of my own billet-doux banged out with a stick on any handy piece of corrugated steel in the ancient language of killing time.

17.

I fall into the ditch or what I think is the ditch. Flat on my back, I stare up at the moon, canvas, sailing above this pleasant seat, my bishopric, and find myself thinking of my kith and kin again and again. The starlight scope is in the car, I hear its honk still, a goose somewhere in the marsh night asking the tower for permission to land. If I had the goggles now, I could see where I've landed but would, more likely, be blinded by this moonlight boosted by the sensitive optics. Night would be day, and the moon over Wapakoneta would be more like the sun over Wapakoneta. I might see some real sun soon if I just close my unaided eyes for a bit and let the whole Ptolemaic contraption overhead wheel and deal.

18.

But the watch I wear is still turned on and on the lookout for pulses of light angling back this way from the fibrillating isotopes atop Pikes Peak. The watch's microprinted works synthesize a "bleep" a second, a steady erosion of my will to doze. At the top of each hour, it drops a drip, and this absence more than the regular tolling pricks me to a semiconducted alertness. The solar panels at the lip of the ditch chirp their chirp, Wapakoneta's moon a dilated pupil centered in each dark iris. And there's the car's snarled sound still hoping to be found. So much for silent night, holy night. Lo, a rocket off yonder rips the raw cloth of night.

19.

At that moment I open my eyes, and in the ditch with me is the big ol' moon its ownself half buried in the mud. Hold on there! There is the moon, the moon over Wapakoneta. It's there up above, where it should be. It's there over this other moon mired in the mud of Wapakoneta. My eyes adjust to the light. O! I'm not in the ditch but on the berm below the old moon museum, the building's geodesic concrete dome, teed up on a dimple in a hummock in

Ohio, mocking the moon overhead. The real moon rises above the arching horizon of this fallen fake.

20.

Armstrong hailed from these Wapakonetish parts. Got drunk here on near beer, I suppose. Contemplated the strobing codes of lightning bugs down by the river. The river caught the moon's pale and silent reflection. Pitched a little woo too. Looked up at the moon, very same moon I spy with my little eye. First guy to go there. Got a pile of rocks marking the spot there. I've seen pictures. "Wish you were here!" Down here they keep the moon rocks he brought back under glass in the hollowed-out moon building before me. The schoolkids, on field trips, herd by the cases of rocks. The little rocks. The big rocks. Big deal! The kids have got a brother or sister, uncles and aunts, sweeping the dust together into neat piles upstairs. Here's to the first man on the moon from the last person on earth.

21.

The earth is slowing down. Friction as it twirls. When the moon untucks the oceans, makes the tides bulge, it's like holding your hand out the car window as you race toward Indiana, a drag against the cool night air, skidding to a halt. Long time coming. Every once in a while, they throw in a leap second or two to bring the world back up to speed. Another cipher of silence at the top of the hour to keep the whole thing in tune. One day the earth will creep to a crawl, and one side will always be facing the face of the moon always facing me. A slow spinning dance around the sun. My watch skips a beat. The silence stretches on and on.

22.

At twelve o'clock high, a huge flock of satellites floats in formation, veiling the moon. They are migrating north. The swallows returning to Capistrano. A new season? Reconnoitering to be done by morning? Who knows? My own orbiting dovecot coos to me still, homing, homing. You are in Ohio, in Wapakoneta, in Ohio.

I release them just like that. The blank LCD goes white in the moonlight. They disperse, disappear, kids playing hide-and-seek in the dark.

23.

At my feet are rocks painted blue by the moon's light. I pick one up out of the dust and launch it into space at the moon hanging over Ohio. I lose sight of it, swallowed up in the intense glare I am aiming at. Sure thing! I've chucked it beyond the bounds of earth. It's slipped into space on the grease of its own inertia. But I hear its reentry, splashing into the ocean of solar panels yards away, the light we've all been staring at turning solid. I heave another sputnik into orbit, hoping to even up the gross mass of the planets that is all out of whack in this binary system. I'm a run-of-the-mill vandal, my slight buzz waning. But soft! A frog jumps into a pond. It makes that sound a frog makes when it jumps into a pond.

24.

Didn't I tell you? It is an hour earlier in Indiana. The moon over Wapakoneta is gaining on me here as I race along the section roads toward home, all of its imaginable phases caught by the thousands and thousands of black reflections in their tropic glass panels. The moon waxes on all the mirrored surfaces, silent, a skipping stone skipping. Yes, I'll catch it tonight as it sets, embrace it, a burned-out pebble, in my empty backyard.

Appliances

DOMESTIC DETAIL AND DESCRIBING RITUALS
OF THE ORDINARY

This craft lecture was first delivered at Warren Wilson College during one of the intense ten-day sessions on the campus in North Carolina when the MFA students meet and attend workshops, readings, classes, and lectures such as this. At the end of the low-residency session, students and teachers return to their homes where the critique of the work continues via the mail.

Narratives from the Crib

As a writer of short fiction, I am interested in the monologue. Recently I discovered a book, *Narratives from the Crib* edited by Katherine Nelson, which is the first extensive study of language acquisition and its relationship to the private babble a child makes before sleep. Other studies of language acquisition are derived, usually, from research done with scripts of conversation between a parent and child. *Narratives from the Crib* is an anthology. The contributors all worked with one extensive transcript of the same child. It's pretty amazing stuff. In her monologue the child does different voices, teaches herself how to talk to herself, rehearses and revises the events of her day, comforts herself with repetition and formula phrases. She dramatizes, and she experiments in exposition.

Those of you who have children or who have been around children know of crib narratives, that singsong speech taking shape before your very ears. Once I thought maybe I could do something with this study, use it to enlighten my ideas about the monologue as a form in fiction. But as I was thinking about my own child's initial attempts at monologue, my thinking took a turn.

I realized I was eavesdropping on my son's primal steps into language. He was teaching himself to speak and doing so in what to him was a space, his nursery, where he experienced his first inkling of privacy. I was suddenly struck then not with his monologue, as I thought I would be, but with the means I used to overhear him utter it. I listened not to my son directly but to a simple little appliance, the baby monitor.

I realized that I had been listening for two years to the private utterances of my son as he fell asleep, as he "read" to himself in his crib, as he addressed his toys, as he sang to the moon. Most of the time it would only be the burbling buzz beneath the drone of the television, emitting its own nonsense where I listened with my wife to both broadcasts. Or I heard him above the clank of cooking sounds. I heard him as I used the phone, his speech a bit of interference like those shadow conversations you hear sometimes on the wires as you talk. Sooner or later those nights, the base station in his room would transmit to the portable receiver I carried around the house the panting exhalation of his sleep breathing. Strangely unable to capture the diastolic inhalation that goes along with the exhalation, the electronics betrayed us as new parents. We found at first that we hung not just on his next word but on his next breath. We held our own breaths until his next breath, until, out of sheer exhaustion of attention, we channeled his sleep sounds into a subordinate track of hearing. We got used to it, and we forgot we lugged around that receiver as we moved around the house. The box, the box became a little breathing thing on my belt. We no longer listened to my son but to the box.

Once I had stumbled into remembering the baby monitor, a device that became an ordinary accoutrement of the modern layette, it now seemed so strange. It also struck me that my parents never had one. How had they "monitored" me? I suppose they looked in on me from time to time if they came upstairs, but here I am guessing. It never occurred to them to rig up some listening device. I asked them that. But now the monitor has become standard field equipment delivered in the showers before delivery. Now it is necessary.

The Invention of the Dishwasher

Does this appearance of a new technology, however slight, change anything significant in the world? Or, more for my purposes here, do the appearances of such technologies change the world of stories?

The quick answer is, "Yeah, sure," and then move on. Another brief answer is that these machines are so prevalent now as to have become invisible, and their effects, if there are effects at all, are minor. But I began thinking about the presence of such machines in my own life and the way they appear and do work in the stories I write or read.

In many stories I read, appliances are often deployed neutrally, salting the setting with status detail, class-marking the kitchen or living room. Appliances usually are no more than a part of the landscape in which characters have evolved, and so characters' physiognomies have already absorbed and incorporated what influences emanate from such machines. Appliances are used mainly as scenery, a way to indicate the historic time of the story, a way to fill up space or background, things, merely, to run or handle, props, business for the character to perform when the real action is happening between people. I am interested here in the character of these machines, their secret histories and their ability to influence, subtly and profoundly, that action happening between people, real and imagined.

Take the invention of the dishwasher. The dishwasher, according to my notes, was first invented in 1924 by a woman in

Shelbyville, Indiana. You would think, perhaps, that her motivation for inventing the machine was to escape the drudgery of the task. In fact, she was spurred on by her frustration with her servants. They broke her fine china.

Once loosed upon the world, of course, a machine takes on valences its inventor cannot anticipate, could not have even imagined. We did not have servants in my family. We all washed dishes after sit-down family meals. Until we got a machine. At the same time, it seems, we also began to eat separately, loading our individual dishes separately, storing them in the racks until there was a load to do.

The columnist Ellen Goodman once mused on the introduction of innocuous Velcro and the disruption it had caused in the relationship between her and her children's children. The grandparent's task of instructing grandchildren in the art of tying shoes had been disrupted. The concentrated effort and shared time it took to coach a child through elemental knotting had been diminished, if not eliminated altogether, and with it, she concludes, the knotting of the relationship.

The Effect of the Blender upon the Great Verities

This drama with machines and new gadgetry is continuous. It certainly is nothing new to the Amish, whose quaint ways represent a feisty consciousness of the potential of material technology to disrupt relationships and patterns of culture they privilege. They constantly explore the ramifications of things that become "everyday." There are a lot of new things that now become "everyday" every day. What is the big deal, after all, with the preference for a hook and eye and the shunning of a button?

Strange, when I talk about the Amish with others, they usually erupt with anecdotal evidence of backsliding by the Amish. "They use cars. They use telephones. I've seen them watch TVs in hotel lobbies." These accusations are more interesting in what they say about us, not the Amish, and our relationship with cars, telephones, and TVs than what they reveal about the Amish. Our response implies that the presence of such machines in our lives, when we *do* think about it, is anything but neutral. We imagine those machines as irresistible, as possessing in themselves a power over us that erodes even the most pious. We can't *help* using these machines once they are here. But suggest that this is the case, and the same informants will argue that in matters of importance in our lives gadgets and gizmos do not really affect us profoundly, that the great verities go unaffected when they come into contact with a blender. There is always this denial, the belief or the desire that the presence of technologies is benign at least or, at most, manageable. Fatalistically, we sigh. The cat's out of the bag; the genie's out of the bottle. "That's progress!" What are you going to do about it?

It seems I am making this an issue of fasteners. What does the appearance of Velcro have to do with how we attach ourselves to each other? It is also a matter of the walls and doorways of our interior space and the collecting clutter of devices of convenience that occupy the rooms in which we convene.

A Digression on the Domestic Landscape

I would like to muse further on this relationship to relationships, how human drama is interfered with, warped if you will, by the electromagnetic fields of small home appliances. But first I want to stray a bit. I would like this meandering meditation here to make strange again the ordinary and everyday in order to put a kind of life back into objects and to have these newly strange objects in-form in interesting ways the lives of characters. So I would like to begin with the house itself, a kind of big machine for our own living and, very often, the contraption housing characters and their interactions.

In *The Most Beautiful House in the World*, Witold Rybczynski considers Pieter Brueghel the Elder's painting *Children's Games* and counts in it almost a hundred different examples of juvenile play. There are representations of blindman's bluff, marbles, jacks, and dolls that we would recognize today some four hundred years after they were painted. What is missing, he points out, are building games. Except for a pile of actual bricks, arranged slightly and abandoned in the corner of Brueghel's 1560 painting, construction toys or the act of simulated building does not appear. Though Rybczynski doesn't mention it one way or the other, the painting also fails to show the acts of reading and/or writing, adult forms of play.

Rybczynski traces the appearance of building games to later paintings where houses of cards indicate the first construction plaything, and he notes that the notion of play is changing as well. Play is becoming specialized. Games before were readily played by both adults and children. However, he finds that Milton, perhaps the earliest example, uses the metaphor of play in a way that implies it is solely a child's pastime. Indoor toys—lead soldiers, clockwork toys, jigsaw puzzles, doll's houses—appear at this time.

"Seventeenth century Holland where domesticity first developed we see children playing in the home, alone. When play moved indoors it not only became more private, it changed in disposition. Outdoor games were boisterous, noisy and usually rowdy. . . . It takes long periods of quiet concentration to build a house of cards and the availability of this time signals the growing isolation and introspection of child's play."

H. G. Wells points out in a monograph on indoor games that one needs a floor before one can play indoors. One needs a house, as we know it, before one can build a model of a house. It was only recently, in 1837, that Friedrich Froebel, the father of kindergarten, first built building blocks. In the 1910s, toys using miniaturized versions of actual building materials were developed, the Erector Set, for example, Tinker Toys, and also Lincoln Logs, which were invented by Frank Lloyd Wright's son. LEGOs appeared in 1949.

The point is that this domestic landscape we now take for granted is relatively new and still under construction, and is connected, in interesting ways, to play and to class and to wealth, to material, to social history. Note that the very nature of house, the domesticity as it has evolved, has favored privacy, isolation, and specialization. Rooms acquired, and are still acquiring, special characteristics — bedroom, bathroom, kitchen — and the house itself has become a place separate from work, though it is becoming a place where work is once again performed but now in specialized home offices, dens, media rooms. The contemporary tendency in most cases is in part due to the appearance of certain new appliances — computers, modems, fax machines — which have fuzzed, once again, the distinction of where we work and where we live.

In one drawing of our house that my son did before he went to school, he placed me in the little triangle space at the top, beneath the roof, a room he calls "The Cloud Room," the attic really, which is now my office, where I am at this moment working on this essay. There I am in his picture, typing away on my computer in the drawing of our house he did in his own room a floor below.

The Storied House

Do you have a "storied" house? I have in my mind a house that is constructed and stored in my memory and ready to accommodate any story I stumble upon.

I find that when I read a story that begins by establishing its setting in a house or even a flat or apartment, I picture in my mind first, before details in the particular story I am reading amend the vision, the interior of a house at 1730 Spring Street in Fort Wayne, Indiana. I lived there from the time I was two until I was twelve. It is the house in which my mother read to me and in which I learned to read. It is the house in which for me all stories begin.

Reading a story always renovates the house template somewhat as I go along, but it is fortunate that the house I am stuck with is of the type that was already highly adaptable, conceived that way by its architects and builders. Its design is akin to all the mass production methods employed at the time. That is, it is a standard base model with an array of options. The house that is my storied house, then, is already a kind of machine and a machined thing. The house as appliance. The kind catalog stores loaded up on a rail flatcar and shipped to the sticks.

The house at 1730 Spring is a foursquare house, a design popular in the teens and twenties, available as a kit from Sears, Roebuck. Its footprint on the lot is a perfect square. That square is mirrored in its elevation as a cube. As you might guess, each floor plan of each house is remarkably diverse as the walls divide and subdivide the space into smaller squares and rectangles almost like Japanese sliding panels. Rooms and permutations of rooms.

In forty years, I have lived in fourteen houses. Four of them, including the one I am living in now, have been foursquare houses. So the foursquare house model itself allows for easy rearranging of space and rooms, and my history allows me to shunt from one house to another in my past to find the best match to the needs of my imagination. I move from 1730 Spring Street to 519 Northwestern in Ames, Iowa, to 348 Fellows in Syracuse, New York, effortlessly lugging the occupants of the story with me to the new venue, a cozier fit.

I find it is very hard for a story, any story, to overwhelm this interior space hardwired in my head. I am reminded of the mnemonic device of placing text you want to remember in rooms and closets and nooks of a vast building. There is a space inside you that contains *the* space, an architecture of memory. The space you know by heart.

The first practical and nonmilitary adaptation of virtual reality imaging was in computer-assisted design (CAD) that allowed architects to walk through buildings before they were built. This virtual reality is, for me, old hat. It has always been the reality of reading for me.

Vladimir Nabokov as Interior Decorator

Nabokov, perhaps to undo the default house map he carried around inside his head, rendered a detailed floor plan of the Samsa flat in Kafka's *Metamorphosis*. His visualization of the space is crucial to his reading of the story, in which he sees structure in a triad of threes. The three body segments of the insect, the three humans left in the family, the three boarders, etc. He doesn't want to make too much of this, wishing "to limit the Kafka symbol of three to its aesthetic and logical significance and disregard whatever myths the sexual mythologists read into it under the direction of Viennese witch doctors." He carefully notes there are three rooms and three communicating doors that are constantly opening and closing throughout the whole story. In short, it is crucial for us, says Nabokov, to know the setting of the story in order to understand the story.

For setting I like to substitute the phrase "ground situation," a phrase cribbed from my former writing teacher. It implies that there is more in the background than just scenery. That "the setting" is really integrated into the situation of the characters, that the characters are part of the setting, not just placed before it.

What is it about the house that makes it such a charged landscape? That gives it such potential as a place a story can take place?

For me the house, as I have been thinking about it here, is a place that simultaneously contains extreme intimacy and extreme isolation. The house excites us, as we read or write, as the vessel for arenas of privacy and the precinct of public space where intimates discover secrets about each other or strive to keep secrets from each other.

Nabokov's sneer aside, it is amusing to assume that Freud needed this kind of space to exist in order to theorize about privacy and intimacy and family. No Freud until we have rooms. A house divided against itself not only stands but is also an interesting house. And it is not that big a leap to argue that practices of fiction reading and writing correspond in their development directly to the development of the middle-class detached home. The naturalist Frank Norris, also a sneerer, dismisses W. D. Howells, Henry James, and Edith Wharton as practitioners of the fiction that finds tragedy "in a broken teacup." Indeed.

A house, with its many chambers, begins with the promise of privacy and intimacy as well as privacy from intimacy. It promises escape in many forms and sudden exposure and discovery. The house, this evolved domestic landscape, dictates organically the drama it contains.

Machines of Loving Grace

I had a friend who went to museum school in Washington, D.C. Her subject area was the kitchen. The controversy at George Washington then—it might still be one now—was the application of labels, the labeling of artifacts, displays, exhibits. Should those texts be affixed next to the object? Why should they be used? Beneath these questions were others that concern the nature of the museum experience. How should the viewer be placed in relationship to the objects viewed? Is the purpose of the bellows vacuum cleaner—its use, its workings, its significance—self-evident? Should a visitor contemplating the mystery of an antique cherry pitter be instructed or be allowed to discover? On both sides of these issues, however, is the assumption that something has gone out of the artifact. It is dead to us now because our relationship to it has been severed by time or obsolescence, a change of circumstance.

Strangely, many of these objects often do come back to us, reanimated but in new ways. Their emotional content now is divorced from function. They are fetishes, collectibles. The windmill in the yard. The tools on the wall. The butter churn with flowers. And they have another kind of life with us in our homes.

It is difficult for us to see how machines live and how our lives relate to machines. Our initial response, I suppose, is that most are simple substitutions for what existed previously. We just hooked up a motor. The reality is more complicated.

Along with crib narratives, I also study black box narratives. Those would be the transcripts taken from the flight recorders of airplanes as they crash. The black boxes are not black, of course. They are usually orange or yellow. The recorders record a heightened interaction between people and complex machines, in this case airplanes. But I entertain the parallel that much domestic fiction can be thought of as a kind of black box narrative, tracking information as the inhabitants tail into the ground or come in for a safe landing. We are the ghosts or souls in these machines of our making. Yes, you can think of the house evolving into such a machine. We daily live now with several cybernetic systems — the thermostats in our furnaces and hot water heaters and refrigerators. Coffee machines that turn themselves on. Self-cleaning ovens. Not quite as smart as the house in the Ray Bradbury story but getting there.

I am curious about the ways we communicate with these large, complex systems. There is a vast array of controls in an airplane. Flight recorder data has shown that flight officers' inability to find an instrument in the busy array of dials and toggles has many times caused crashes. In response to past disasters, we now mark the landing gear control by a lever topped with a little wheel, the flaps by a lever with wings, etc., so that the instrument panel of an airplane begins to look something like a baby's busy box.

The crew either knows or doesn't know of the impending disaster. There is a certain poignancy and irony in the latter versions. You can hear the flight officers talking. Often they are talking about what is going on at home, often right up to the moment of impact. Planes fly themselves. But also you hear the voice of the plane, the warnings it announces that the crew ignores because they are engrossed in the domestic drama they believe they are flying home to.

We might all pay more attention to the machines that talk to us while we are talking or that allow us to talk, or record our voice or our words. There are a lot of them now, those appliances that have the most potential to disrupt the relationships at play, the secrets intimates keep from one another, in the domestic landscape.

The baby monitor with which I easily eavesdropped on my son altered my relationship with him. Or more precisely it was part of the relationship I have with my son. Or more precisely it *was* my relationship with my son.

In Piaget's famous experiments, he mapped the lines of development in humans. For a baby at a certain age, a ball that rolls out of sight is out of mind, forgotten. A little older, and the same baby can remember that the ball exists even out of sight. In my own development as a parent, the monitor never allowed me to put my son out of my mind. He was always there even while out of sight. Who's to say how this particular rearranging of space and time, these electronic apron strings, will shape my relationship with my son? Or who's to say what the cumulative effect to our culture is, a whole generation and class of children raised with the imposition of the device?

The Machines from Syracuse

In the summers when I teach at Warren Wilson, I am assigned a classroom in a specific building because the classroom and the building are air-conditioned. I can think of quite a few sticky summer days on which it would have been impossible to proceed without this chilled space. It is the appliance that makes possible my serious deliberations with my students. And allow me to recall for you here the little dance that goes on in that classroom, with someone getting up to fiddle with the blower, to adjust the thermostat, the temperature never quite right. A machine creates the environment in which my students and I consider the art and craft of fiction writing. Without it, we might merely repair to the veranda.

The Carrier Corporation developed the first practical air-conditioning system and did so in Syracuse, New York, a place famous for its snow and mild summers. The reason the machine was invented was to make it possible to better automatically weave fabric in the South. The first air conditioners lowered the humidity in the mills so that the knitting machines, other machines, would be comfortable. The design did not really take into account the comfort of the human operators. But people were already involved with those weaving machines. And machines have lives of their own, as we have seen. And that box transformed the South. It is impossible now to imagine the South without it and by extension impossible to imagine the new fiction of the South without it.

Syracuse was also once called Typewriter City. Royal, Smith, Corona, Underwood, all were there. The last factory, a Smith-Corona one, has just closed and headed to Mexico. I walk the streets of my neighborhood on trash day and search for old portable typewriters abandoned to the garbage. I am fond of a particular model, the one I learned to type on. It's from the forties, maroon enamel. I have four of them now and some Zephyr laptops from the thirties. I can be choosy, there are so many of them on the curb. Hundreds heading to the dump. As I crouch there testing the workings of one, I wonder about the house from which the machine came. What did it mean to have a typewriter around and not use it? Most of these machines show little wear. I wonder whether they have been replaced or if the existence of the computer has just allowed owners to admit they don't use a typewriter and can rid themselves of any writing machine. I don't know.

And I've noticed recently that writers don't ask each other so much anymore if they use a computer. The pencil question might still be a possibility, but the machine question has been settled. If we use a machine, chances are we are quarreling over system software, not hardware. And why do we ask those types of questions anyway if we don't believe appliances play a major role in our lives and the way we think and the way we think about life and in the way we work and the way we make our work?

I, Computer

I asked my son to interpret his drawing, the drawing of our house, the one with me up in the attic office working at my desk. What am I doing in the Cloud Room? He looked at me, trying to figure out the trick. He knows I am a "writer"—I have even visited his kindergarten class to talk about my job as a "writer"—but what is a "writer" anyway? He answered as if it were obvious, and it was. "You're computing," he said, and I am.

The History of Corn

When I give craft lectures like this one, I like to produce handouts. In this case, they were reproductions of the post office murals I describe. The lecture was first delivered at Warren Wilson.

Above the postmaster's door, you see a picture of one kernel of corn. It hangs there as large as a side of beef and painted in those tequila sunrise hues, yellow blending to orange shading to a reddish brown, that are also the stripes of candy corn. At the same time, you can see into the seed through a heart-shaped cutaway, into the germ coiled there heart-shaped as well, white and shiny, the actual size of a small animal brain. Foiling the kernel, adding to the rounded relief of the swelling, the fertile grain, is a thicket of cornstalks sewn so close together the leaves and silk and ears weave into a knobby burlap background. The tops of the stalks you can only imagine, tasseling way above where the canvas has run out through the ceiling, up into the congressional office upstairs, while the roots root the way corn does, a lace of flying buttresses tenting out from the telescoping stalks and into the rich mahogany crust of earth that turns into the mahogany trim of the postmaster's door and the flanking frames of bulletin boards tacked with wanted posters and blowups of newly issued stamps.

The mural is called *The History of Corn,* and it was painted in 1938 by Lowell Houser as part of the Treasury Department's

Section of Fine Arts. The post office is on Kellogg Street, yes that Kellogg, in Ames, Iowa. And as I used to stand in line at the window, staring up at the mural, I could feel the vibrations through the ground of the mile-long grain trains, covered hoppers painted the colors of after-dinner mints, dragging through a crossing two blocks away. An atmosphere of corn.

The composition of the mural is symmetrical. There are two similar images on either side of the giant kernel. On the left side, in hieroglyphic profile, is a shirtless Aztec farmer, angled at the waist, scratching at a hill of corn with a flint-tipped digging stick. On the other side an Iowa farmer is grubbing at the base of a plant looking for cutworm. His posture too is Egyptian, though he is dressed in blue bib overalls and a crushed engineer's hat. They both are bowing toward the painting's center while over their shoulders, in the upper corners, their respective suns shine down, one with a pre-Columbian visage, the other rendered more realistically but still tattooed with a scientific swatch of the visible spectrum. In the lower corners, the theme continues. A squat, carved god is balanced by the crouched black-enameled microscope. The skyline of stepped pyramids and balconied temples reflects the setbacks of the skyscrapers and the grain elevator bandoleer. There, a string of feathers and semiprecious stones coils at the farmer's feet, and there, a ticker tape snakes through the grass, a cousin plant that the corn evolved from. On that tape, in the code of numbers and letters, you can read LH 38, the artist's signature.

What better place for writers to consider stories than in the lobbies of the post offices, the launching pads for their manila-clad space shuttles whose three-month missions are to explore strange new worlds then return to them on the desert landing strips of their desks. The calculus of delivery times, the sixth sense of sensing, yes, this is less than twelve ounces, priority rate. The naive simple trust in this country of the tongue not only to create the language but also to lick the stamp to get it there.

Chances are you know of one of these murals. Between 1934 and 1943 the Fine Arts Section of the Treasury Department commissioned more than 1,100 post office murals; 1,000 still exist. Or at least you have a sense of their style if you know the Revolutionary Muralists of Mexico, Rivera or Orozco, from which much of the post office work derived, or the regionalist school of Curry, Benton, and Wood, or any of the painting and poster art thrown into the social realist category.

I am interested in these pictures because they are predominantly narrative. I think we can learn some things from the paintings that might inform the writing of stories. But I am also interested in the other meaning of corn—the cornball, the kitschy—a succotash we mostly avoid placing on our menus. These pictures of local products and industry, of local history and politics perhaps seem quaint to us now, their content and messages wrong-headed if not dead-ended, the emotion just plain corny. I am here to introduce to you the history of this corn, suggest to you that the motives and the conflicts that powered this art still concern us. As Park and Markowitz point out in their book *Post Offices and Public Art in the New Deal:*

> There were tensions between three polarities: the desire for quality in
> art and the commitment to make art democratic; the effort to make art
> embodying national ideas and values and the wish to make art relevant
> to people in various regions of the country; traditional artistic values
> and contemporary styles.

Our art still passes through the lobbies of these strange symbolic precincts, physically and metaphorically, where these polarities are still tussling. We may not think of ourselves as social realists but neither do we participate in its opposite. What would that be? Capital irrealists? And what is an example of capital irrealism? Commercials, I guess. Writing and reading are intensely private acts. I hope that thinking about these public murals we will be nudged a ways toward consideration of our greater cultures, our larger communities. I hope that we will become more comfortable as a culture incorporating in our fictions the social, the political, the historical and risk a more public display of private emotion.

In the last twenty years much has been made of the use of fictional techniques in nonfiction writing. I guess here I will be asking you to think of it the other way around, the nonfiction in the fiction.

To do that we must focus on the ground situation, my teacher's name for an enriched setting, not just the physical details of place and time but how a certain place and time adds to the physics of characters in conflict, the tensions inherent in any human situation. To write, as a New Testament storyteller narrates, "Once there was a man who had two sons" is to establish this ground situation without much setting at all. The perceptive reader senses instantly the vectors of generational and filial conflict inherent in the relationship. Those vectors aren't elaborated but understood. The story begins when those bonds, under the given pressure, break.

This break is often marked by the phrase "one day." "One day the youngest son came to his father and said: I am leaving. Give to me all that is owed. I plan to make my way in the world." We know that we have read a story when we can return to that original ground situation and feel that the valences of those relationships are now different. By comparing the change in the ground, we judge what has happened.

To visualize this I like to conjure up the picture of those party games of wooden blocks piled into a tower or painted disks squeezed together in a frame by a spring plunger. You know, these games where the players then try to remove the blocks or disks without disturbing the architecture of the overall construction. There comes the turn when every block or disk, compacted or extended, is contributing to the precarious stability of the whole. No piece can be disturbed without setting off the chain reaction of gravity or elasticity. This then seems like a great model for the moment to begin a story. The ground situation enriched the way uranium is enriched: a landscape saturated with such people

and places in stress, held together with mutual tension and re-
vulsion.

But in writing a story, because it is, after all, short, you don't
often have the option of the two-step construction—you can't
build the tower to then make it fall down. In a short story you are
doing both tasks simultaneously. You are creating the matter as it
is being consumed. While you murder, you create.

A critic felt, while regarding Thomas Hart Benton's *America Today*
murals, that he was "looking out of the window of a train speed-
ing through cities, past factories and mines, through farmland and
woods, over prairies, across rivers. They convey a sense of the
restless, teeming, tumultuous life of this country, its wide range
of contrast, and its epic proportions." The ground situation of a
story wraps itself around the hurtling private compartment of plot,
its main line of gesture and event. It should always be there in the
periphery—informing, foiling, stoking the energy and the action
of the intimate human drama that is, at once, part of the scenery
and passing through it.

You can see a good example of this capillary exchange through
the membrane that separates background and action in the way
Benton has composed the political speech panel of his mural *A
Social History of the State of Missouri*. Set deep in the panel is a
dominating, grim poster: a political candidate framed with bun-
ting. On the stage before the poster, a speaker gesticulates grandly.
The audience leans in to hear. You see the audience from behind.
Their bald spots, their shiny Sunday suit jackets too small and
tight across their shoulders. On the backbench a woman has
turned away from the speaker, toward you. The bodice of her dress
unbuttoned. Has she just finished nursing the baby, bare-assed,
butt up, on her lap, that she is now wiping clean to re-diaper?

These murals attempt, by the design of hundreds of details, to
convey the simultaneous presence of the historic and social life of
the greater community with the personal specific struggle of a protagonist. Purely as a practical matter, placing stories in such fertile
media will make it easier for things to happen, for characters to do

things. Every bit of the canvas contains potential. The gun on the wall becomes the gun in the hand; the scenic becomes the scene. But beyond that, this interaction of setting simply feels right, is right for the way we feel the real world.

Auden, in his poem "Musée des Beaux Arts," reminds us of such things. Referring to Brueghel's "Icarus," he pictures the way to picture suffering: "Its human position; how it takes place / While someone else is eating or opening a window or just walking dully along." And that innocent behind the torturer's horse is scratching recalls the baby in Benton's painting where you can see the soiled diaper thrown in the wicker basket by the mother's feet. And next to the mother and baby, other women are preparing a lunch of iced cake and sandwiches taken from the same style willow hampers. And, there, over their shoulders in the far distance a little speck of a lynched man in a tree. The event no bigger than Icarus's white legs disappearing into the sea.

Let me try to picture some examples of post office murals. I sort them into three rough categories in order to talk about them. But what should be noticed about all of these pictures, the next time you look, is how crammed they are with things, how busy they are. These murals seem to be telling two types of stories simultaneously. Any one of the figures has his or her own story, while at the same time those stories are embedded in the larger story of the whole painting. This tension, one of the polarities Park and Markowitz discuss, gives these murals, in my mind, their charm and power. And it is this very tension I puzzle over when writing my own stories or reading the stories of others. How to engage both spheres of the characters' lives and locales—the private and public, the microcosmic and the cosmic.

The first group of murals seems to be concerned with stories of social interaction. Stuyvesant Van Veen's *Pittsburgh Panorama* places people in the foreground, but it is the intricacy of mass construction, the sweep of the city spread out below them that dominates.

Still, my eye is drawn to the one figure at the left on the high bridge spanning the width of the picture who sits dangling a leg over the railing. The painting reverses the cliché of people viewed as ants from the top of a tall building. Instead the people nearest us are still ant-size. They look down upon the Brio landscape of their city as it turns into repeating abstract forms. The panorama, the comprehensive view, puts the city in place, returns it to a human scale while at the same time recording its vastness. The individual stories are undercut while their collective creation still does not overwhelm.

Harry Sternberg's Balthus-like family picnics allegorically in the negative of the same industrial landscape in his Ambler, Pennsylvania, mural called *The Family — Industry and Agriculture*. It is a pastoral without the pasture and without the ton of people used as scenery. Only the residue of their work remains. The nuclear family, a mom and dad and baby, clings to their life-raft quilt, floating on a patch of grass and buttercups. They cling to each other in a complicated, almost Egyptian embrace. They look like they are touching base. They are estranged from and responsible for the kind of desert that surrounds them, repeating images of smokestacks and cabbages in rows. The man and woman frozen into machined angles blend into the machined shapes around them. Only the baby retains a bit of organic roundness, but he is speared by the tines of his father's fingers. Oh unhappy family, fruit of what marriage?

The second grouping records the same type of social dynamic but adds the dimension of time. These historical murals either allow you to see through the layers of time, as in "The Story of Venice" or the dozens of other "The Story of . . ."s or "The History of Corn," or picture the historical instant, as in the "Invention of the Paper Bag in Canajoharie" rendered by Anatol Shulkin for the town of Canajoharie, New York. It records, in epic grandeur and in seemingly non-ironic terms, a medieval clutch of workers posed in adoration as if huddled around the manger where, instead of a baby, a paper bag rests beatifically. Again the desire is to connect individual action to the sweep of larger forces. Time is another depth to the portrait.

I call the final grouping documentary. These murals often imply the desire to capture the social and historical forces converging on the moment of the mural's actual creation but also the recognition of the artist's responsibility to record the feeling of the present time.

I have this wonderful regional cookbook at home published in 1948. In it the authors spend two pages introducing a new vegetable, or reintroducing it since it was popular, the text says, in colonial times. The vegetable is broccoli. In 1948 it was as exotic as arugula or Fuji pears in more recent times.

I think of this when I look at the modern *Suburban Street* by Alan Tompkins for an Indianapolis post office. The grocer holds a wood crate. A ham hangs in the window along with several hands of bananas. The buggy and the bicycle are so old now, their designs on the edge of our knowing them. Look, the man actually knew the letter carrier well enough to get his mail on the street. The whole scene doesn't even look like a suburban street as we think of it today. People are on the streets. There are no cars. These are the kinds of details writers must pay special attention to as they work in their own times. It is the usual consciousness that aims for a timelessness and universality. It is important to include the immediate as well.

Remember the man in Gatsby's library commenting on how the pages of the books hadn't been cut. Or in the Hemingway story called "The Killers," a customer in the diner orders his food "to go." The quotation marks suggest this was a new idea at the time. This is the neat stuff of everyday life that needs to be rendered as it is here in these paintings. The power of the photos of Berenice Abbott for me stems from her time*ful*ness.

A fact is a thing done. Fiction is a thing made, and the things painters and writers create will exist long after the model is extinct—the rotary telephone, the safety pin, the bottle cap, the 45 (the gun and the disk of vinyl). A story then should not only contain a sense of the history leading to the moment of the telling but a sense that, as it is told, it too becomes a historical artifact. Stories are fictions but also facts of a particular time.

"So I have sailed the seas and come . . . to B . . . a small town fastened to a field in Indiana."

So begins William Gass's story, "In the Heart of the Heart of the Country." And here is something corny. After I read that story for the first time in college, a group of us from class piled into Michael Wilkerson's Gremlin and went looking for the town, B., using the details of the story as a field guide for our search. Beanblossom, Bloomington, Bedford, Battleground. Battleground, we liked it just for the name. Brookston. We think it was Brookston.

> Down the back streets the asphalt crumbles into gravel. There's Westbrook's with the geraniums, Horsefall's, Mott's. The sidewalk shatters. Gravel dust rises like the breath behind the wagons. And I am in retirement from love.

Gass's story seems as if it were constructed like the murals we've looked at. It is made up of short patches of prose, each with its own title — A PLACE, MY HOUSE, WEATHER, POLITICS, VITAL DATA. There are thirty-six of these little stories in all. Some of these titles are repeated. Sometimes they are combined to form a new title — MY HOUSE, THIS PLACE AND BODY. Sometimes a story is continued from one section to another, leapfrogging four or five other sections, and sometimes not. The effect is that confusion between foreground and background. The strategy is to attain a critical mass simply from the accumulation of details. We experience the story in the same way the drowsing Emperor, alluded to at the beginning, experiences the music box. "In the Heart of the Heart of the Country" is a kind of mechanical, gilded bird, jeweled, geared, intricate enough, it is hoped, to come alive. And the story lives in a way the real town of Brookston does not. It has its timelessness. Though it faithfully replicates and documents, it ultimately transforms itself into something else entirely.

The narrator has come to the small town, he says, to avoid love and to write poetry about it. But his eye is drawn to what surrounds him, and he writes the poetry of estrangement by recording his estrangement. This is the story of the overall canvas. But, as in the murals I've mentioned, there are many other splotches of stories, side altars, skirmishes that together make the cathedral or the battle.

The sections shift in tone. Overall the story could read like a handbook of rhetoric. But the reasonable voice explodes from time to time, a Tourette-like syndrome, into an excruciating utterance:

> I have met with some mischance, wings withering, as Plato says obscurely, and across the breadth of Ohio, like heaven on a table, I've fallen as far as the poet, the sixth sort of body, this house in B, in Indiana.

> There is little hand in hand here . . . not in B. No one touches except in rage. Occasionally girls will twine their arms about each other and lurch along, school out, toward home and play. I dreamed my lips would drift down your back like a skiff on a river. I'd follow a vein with the point of my finger, hold your bare feet in my naked hands.

The reader here is mostly addressed as student, a student who turns suddenly into student lover.

The story uses all forms of nonfiction voices — scholarly essay, guidebook prose, chamber of commerce pamphlet, phone book litany:

> "The Modern Homemakers" Demonstration Club. The Prairie Home Demonstration Club. The Night-outer's Home Demonstration Club. The IOOF, FFF, VFW, WCTU, WSCS, 4-H, 40 and 8, Psi Iota Chi, and PTA. The Boy and Girl Scouts, Rainbows, Masons, Indians and Rebekah Lodge.

Gossip introduces a historical figure the way Rivera painted Lenin into the mural at Rockefeller Center:

I've heard Batista described as a Mason. A farmer who'd seen him in Miami made this claim. He's as nice a fellow as you'd ever want to meet. Of Castro, of course, no one speaks.

This too is a detail of the timefulness of the writing. And here is the voice of the newspaper editorialist:

Many small Midwestern towns are nothing more than rural slums, and this community could easily become one.

"In the Heart of the Heart of the Country" is a story about the ground situation. From the squared blocks of prose that pictorially map the grid of the small town streets to the scraps of language Gass pastes into the collage, the story is constructed in such a way that the change takes place once it is all taken in. The reader is to be pulled in by the preponderance of the evidence he or she has been sifting through. As you read, the details fall like snow that suddenly is ash. The character is clearly visible once he is coated, like a statue in the town square after such a storm, with a film of detail.

Let me take a second to look at what I call "the stare" in stories. A great stare comes at the end of Joyce's "The Dead" as Gabriel stares out the window and watches the snow, recalling a weather report description of the event. Snow was general all over Ireland. "The Dead" is a story with lots of ground. What really happens? They go to a party. Someone sings. His wife remembers something. It changes his life. The story lives in the complex layering in the periphery. The few events reorder, genetically reorder, the code of his landscape. And we watch as he stares at that world transformed.

I love the stare. Mrs. Turpin's in Flannery O'Connor's "Revelation." Nick looking at the swamp in "Big Two-Hearted River." The two couples looking at the table at the end of "What We Talk about When We Talk about Love." Rick staring at the legal pad in Ron Hansen's "Can I Just Sit Here Awhile?" I love the stare. We, the readers, stare at them staring, and through them we see (no, not see, because it is as if the eyes of the characters have been rendered inoperative, the eyes only outposts now for a whole array of sensing apparati), we feel the frequency shift, the harmonics pitched differently, the new disturbances in the field.

I am reminded of science fiction movies where the actors do a lot of staring. At monitors on the spaceship, say, where they see something horrible, a monster, a star exploding. It must be hard to act in such movies. You know, the director yells that this or that is happening, but the actors react to a blank space. The special effects will be added later. The actors stare at blue screens and try to conjure up something on their inner screens that will make them quake.

"In the Heart of the Heart of the Country" seeks to cut out the middleman. It is the special effect. It replaces Gabriel Conroy with a narrator that speaks inside your head. The reader does—you do—the staring. The story is closer to the way we stare at a mural, the way the faces in the mural, ultimately descendants of the Byzantine icon, stare back at us.

In Christian orthodoxy the icon is thought of not as a picture but more as a window or screen into the spiritual plane. You look into the saintly realm through the eyes of the saint or god who looks back into you, into your inner landscape. Grant Woods's *American Gothic* and these murals tap into the power of such staring, though they are diminished, secular versions. As we have seen, stories too seek to focus vision in a still moment in order to have a vision. In stories like "In the Heart of the Heart of the Country," that crystalline moment is extended as far as it will go. The moment is extended by means of recapitulation, in small sections, the story of the whole. It is a physics of fractals.

Here is an example of such recapitulation:

THE CHURCH

Friday night. Girls in dark skirts and white blouses sit in ranks and scream in concert. They carry funnels loosely stuffed with orange and black paper which they shake wildly, and small megaphones through which, as drilled, they direct and magnify their shouting. Their leaders, barely pubescent girls, prance and shake and whirl their skirts above their bloomers. The young men, leaping, extend their arms and race through puddles of amber light, their bodies glistening. In a lull, though it rarely occurs, you can hear the squeak of tennis shoes against the floor. Then the yelling begins again, and then continues; fathers, mothers, neighbors joining in to form a single pulsing ululation—a cry of the whole community—for in this gymnasium each body becomes the bodies beside it, pressed as they are together, thigh to thigh, and the same shudder runs through all of them, and runs toward the same release. Only the ball scarcely speaks but caroms quietly and lives in peace.

The recorded vision of the narrator binds together the community while his eye is still on the ball. This small satellite is connected to but removed from the larger mass, its puny gravitation disrupting or amplifying the attractive forces of the town. This is the story of this one section. And it is the story of the story. The small voice of the narrator caroms quietly around the town. The story is retold, over and over, from such reordering of details in play.

Roger Angell has pointed out that the pastoral game of baseball is the only sport where the ball doesn't do the scoring. Considering the field, you must simultaneously see the ball in play and the runners running the bases. We follow many smaller stories while we still comprehend the larger one.

It is this simultaneity of events, on planes in several dimensions, regarded by the encompassing stare of a mediating consciousness that works if this kind of story is to work.

And now another "muraled" story from the Midwest:

Down in D-3 I watch the sky gunning through the aperture ninety-odd feet above my head. The missiles are ten months away, and I am lying on my back listening to the sump. From the bottom of a hole, where the weather is always the same cool sixty-four degrees, plus or minus two, I like to relax and watch the clouds slide through the circle of blue light. I have plenty of time to kill. The aperture is about fifteen feet wide. About the size of a silver dollar from here. A hawk just drifted by. Eagle. Crow. Small cumulus. Nothing. Nothing. Wrapper.

Rick DeMarinis's "Under the Wheat" is another mural-like story. It too is told in sections. Narrated by a construction worker building the ICBM silos in North Dakota, the story is another pastoral wandering through a landscape studded with the ruins of finished and unfinished public works. This one is even less populated than Gass's small town; the only people in the landscape are ethnic Russians. The missiles to be planted in their wheat fields point over the top of the world, to the motherland. The diction is of the journal. The narrator picking things up, a freelancer by profession, records the weather, his wife's desertion, fishing, his affair with a local woman. He haunts the deserted streets of a ghost town that once housed the workers of a dam project.

> Caught three lunkers today this morning. All over twenty-four inches. It's 7:00 a.m. now and I'm on Ruby Street, the ghost town. The streets are all named after stones. Why I don't know. This is nothing like anything we have on the coast. Karen [his wife] doesn't like the climate or the people and the flat sky presses down on her from all sides and gives her bad dreams, sleeping and awake. But what can I do?

> I'm on Onyx Street, number 49, a two-bedroom bungalow with a few pieces of furniture left in it. There is a chest of drawers in the bedroom, a bed with a rotten gray mattress. There is a closet with a raggedy slip in it. The slip has brown water stains on it that look like burns. In the bottom of the chest is a magazine, yellow with age. Secret Confessions. I can imagine the woman who lived here with her. Not much like Karen at all. But what did she do while her husband was off working on the dam? Did she stand at this window in her slip and wish she was back in Oxnard? Did she cry her eyes out on this bed and think crazy thoughts? Where is she now? Does she think, "This is July 15, 1962, and I am glad I am not in North Dakota anymore?" Did she take long walks at night and not cook? I have an impulse to do something odd, and do it.

Flatness is all. The sky. The land. His speech. It is easy to see how the story's ground situation is so much of the story. He is always looking up or down or through various membranes of time and space. He is dwarfed by the constructed and the natural features of the place.

Here the narrator is fishing on the still surface of the lake created by the dam:

Something takes my hook and strips off ten yards of line then stops dead. Snag. I reel in. The pole is bent double and the line is singing. Then something lets go but it isn't the line because I'm still snagged. It breaks the surface, a lady's shoe. It's brown and white with a short heel. I toss it into the bottom of the boat. The water is shallow here, and clear. There's something dark and wide under me like a shadow on the water. An old farmhouse, submerged when the dam filled. There's a deep current around the structure. I can see fence, tires, an old truck, feed pens. There is a fat farmer in the yard looking up at me, checking the weather, and I jump away from him, almost tipping the boat. My heart feels tangled in my ribs. But it is only a stump with arms.

The current takes my boat in easy circles. A swimmer would be in serious trouble. I crank up the engine and head back. No fish today. So be it. Sometimes you come home empty-handed. The shoe is new, stylish, and was made in Spain.

At the end of the story he is watching a tornado meander across the plain. The mixing of the various realms continues:

I'm standing on the buckled porch of 49 Onyx Street. Myrna [his lover] is inside reading Secret Confessions: "What My Don Must Never Know." The sky is bad. The lake is bad. It will be a while before we can cross back. I knock on the door, as we planned. Myrna is on the bed in the stained, raggedy slip, giggling. "Listen to this dogshit, Lloyd," she says. But I'm not in the mood for weird stories. "I bought you something, honey," I say. She looks at the soggy shoe. "That?" But she agrees to try it on anyway. I feel like my own ghost, bumping into the familiar run-down walls of my house in the middle of nowhere, and I remember my hatred of it. "Hurry up," I say, my voice true as a razor.

The tornado bears down on them. It is a kind of animated absence and is pictured as the hole in the ground, the silo, becoming solid and deadly. In "Under the Wheat" the landscape, the background, is a character, constantly jumping into Lloyd's life, threatening to carry him away. The landscape, too, is stratified into the times of his life, those layers bracketed by the strata of clouds above and the drowned land below.

Glenn Meeter in "A Harvest" abandons the brief sections and employs an endless piano roll narrative in the second person about a man on a cross-country mission—North to South and back this time, not the standard east to west on-the-road haul.

Ah, down here the Mobilgas man speaks softly Southern and you bless the memory of unpainted wooden signs of Pentecostal, Baptists, and Brethren's who replace the Midwest Gothic Lutherans and Catholics and the tight sphinctered Reformed, whose metal advertisements back North always took the shape of shields or arrows. The Methodists have been with you all the way, like the poor, but down here they too build churches of wood not brick, speak slow, live warm and easy like the soft-barked cottonwoods not ranked in rows but sauntering, graceful, following in lazy curves the flow of land and water.

Again, the story here incorporates what is seen. It encapsulates history encapsulating the story.

Life as a recapitulative journey, old age with the freedom of youth, senility as infant: a pleasing thought as you note how evening echoes morning, how in a lush green field cow leaps upon cow, nature performing civilized perversions, nothing new under the sun, as biologists tell of incest and cannibalism among the lower orders and the noble red elk of Scotland abusing himself on a log. A long aching drive through grass and cattle and horses (patiently doubled, head to withers) with the sun in your eyes: you long for darkness though it means the end of the road. Just North of Spencer, where all are ready for bed, a deer rushes up from a ditch in yellow-blue light—the only deer you have ever seen where the sign warns DEER CROSSING, and you fancy it as a glimpse of beyond. Soon crossing the Missouri in dusk, the sun glowing blue like a footlight beneath earth's rim, you'll be an hour from the last stop of all, in total darkness.

Things rush up out of the darkness. The narrator, the you, keeps stitching the country together, the outer world replicating his inner landscape. Meeter keeps going until the journey runs out:

Drowsy, the mind blinks: pheasant in horizontal flight, yellow-ribbed lark, fiery wheat, heavy harvesters, red dirt and white dust, sunlight's stab on glass, gravel, oil, wide Slavic forehead, Grainbelt, Chaplin, Allis-Chalmers, and aloft with the merest effort, a hawk and a boy on a bike, yes you would do it again, touching nothing, learning nothing, doing nothing at all, but my God what a delight, just to travel through.

All of these works have the feel of scope, of breadth and depth. The stories' settings are integral parts of the stories. They come at you, jack lit, like a wall of paint, a wall of sound. And the wall you see right before you hit it has been graffitied, pamphleted and stripped, papered over and peeling, painted and blistered. The walls are solid, full up.

Or notice the layering of time in Joseph Geha's story "Almost Thirty" from his book *Through and Through*.

Or you might look at the way David Foster Wallace incorporates popular culture into the stories of *Girl with Curious Hair*.

Or the way Mary Swander uses folk art in *Driving the Body Back*.

Or note how Jim Heynen in very brief stories employing a multiple protagonist, the boys, begins with Sioux naming tales and the style of Parson Weems and school primers and binds them together quilt-like in *The Man Who Kept Cigars in His Cap*.

Or the way Alyson Hagy casts her characters' emotional battles on the sites of civil war battlefields in the story "The Field of Lost Shoes."

Or Susan Neville's use of historical figures and folk legends in her stories in *Invention of Flight.*

There are ways to create narrative in print that follow the ways narrative is created in paint. In doing so, these authors have nearly overcome the existential paradox of using words. They have sought to achieve a layered moment of time and space in a medium that is relentlessly sequential. It is true that our eyes move across and around the surface of the mural, but the effect of such grand painting is to be struck all at once by the enormity of history and geography bearing down on us at this moment. The authors of printed stories have long exploited the organic strength of the form's nature. Stories build. They rise to a climax. They illustrate consequences. But words, put down one after the other, left to right, up to down, can also occasionally capture the almost infinite, instantaneous texture of life and have the reader absorb it all almost, it appears, all at once.

After Iowa I moved to Medford, Massachusetts, a sleepy little suburb of Boston straddling the banks of the Mystic River.

I loved to look at the mural in the post office there. It is a map of the Atlantic Ocean with the squiggly coast of New England on one side and the nose of Africa on the other. The islands of the Caribbean float above the clerk's head. Connecting them, the painter has drawn a golden triangle. The slave ships were built on the Mystic River, and the Yankees took them out to trade in people and sugar and rum. But the mural, you see, can go beyond the building. Around the corner from the PO there is a plaque on a wall that says "Jingle Bells" was composed on this site. Carols and slaving share the same shores. I walked up the street Paul Revere took. Crossed the river that is the same one the composer crossed to go through the wood to grandmother's house. All of this could be important. But this is not that remarkable. The world is so cluttered with stuff, chock-full with the residue of lives, the traces of stories.

My favorite story about Medford has to do with the gypsy moth that was brought there in hopes of sparking a silk industry and that escaped to plague the nation. Think how that little worm has transformed our landscape, how every local act is connected to all others.

Today, eighty years after the escape in Medford, the story isn't that of silk hammered into sheet-metal girdles around the trunks of dying trees. In the twenties two Boston biologists went to Japan to collect a fungus, the worm's natural enemy. Returning home, they introduced it, this mosaic chip of genetic code, to rewrite the spreading history of the silkworm. And nothing happened. The gypsy moth spread. The biologists died after long, full lives doing other things. A little sliver, this one failure. But two years ago, as the infestation crossed the Mississippi, the unexpected happened. The insects began to die everywhere. The fungus, needing decades to reach a critical mass, now infested the infestation.

Standing in the post office, I stare up at the picture. I am looking through a scrim of silk to another screen of musty moths' wings painted with eyes that stare back. And through the dust of wings to the ripe eruption of a fungus. The dead biologists. The white set sails of the slave ships. The snow on the ground. The happy sleds on the way to grandmother's house.

There is a story here. There is a story out there.

Ruining a Story

This lecture was first given at Warren Wilson College and then published in the inaugural issue of the *Southern Indiana Review* after I had given the lecture again at The Ropewalk Writers Conference in New Harmony, Indiana. The lecture also appeared in the book *Bringing the Devil to His Knees*, edited by Charles Baxter and Peter Turchi.

The following is the first aesthetic argument I can remember having.

I was in the third grade and had just seen, with a group of my friends, the movie *A Hard Day's Night* starring the Beatles. We were much taken with the movie and the Beatles, so we decided to put on a show at Bill Stuckey's house using the garage there because it was the only one we knew that opened automatically. We could employ the door as an impressive and professional curtain, revealing to the neighborhood kids sitting in the driveway our version of a lip-synched concert. Mark Taylor would be Paul. He was left-handed. Bill Stuckey would be Ringo. Slightly more affluent than the rest of us, he had a drum kit along with the mechanized double garage. A quiet kid named Charlie would be George. His perfection in the role is now supported by my inability to remember his last name. And Rick Blaine would be John because he actually had a guitar he could play and was serious about growing up and playing in a band. He still plays in a band today. For reasons that reveal a lot about me then and now, I wanted desperately to be Brian Epstein, the manager.

Together we set about recreating the concert footage we had recently seen, building the set while listening to the music we would pretend to sing. The yin and yang of the Capitol 45 spun on Bill Stuckey's turntable. A stack of records dense as a devil's food cake floated on the spindle. "Love Me Do." "Please Please Me." "She Loves You, Yeah, Yeah, Yeah." As we worked we heard the screams too, imagined our escape routes through the backyard gardens and alleys, our stage overrun before we could get the garage door down, by hysterical little sisters acting their parts in our kooky adventures.

The falling-out with my friends came over the issue of wires. Our imitation microphones, amplifiers, and electric guitars were connected by means of pilfered extension cords of various gauges and colors. Though the cords carried no load and were plugged into painted cardboard boxes and disguised coatracks, my colleagues in the band paid too much attention, in my mind, to safety. They channeled the cords away from traffic patterns, taped kinks down, even ran lengths of cord under throw rugs. My vision of the archetypal scene of the Fab Four included a carpet of crisscrossing wires dangerously coiling around the tapping Beatle boots. Indeed, all those mysterious connecting wires that were the physical residue of the sound generated the power of the image for me. I liked the way they appeared so randomly, so spontaneously, about their own business. The wires were ignored, overlooked. The performance of the band would be so good you wouldn't notice them. But I did notice.

I couldn't convince the band, the parental lessons of electricity running too deep perhaps. Besides, it didn't matter. The shake of Ringo's head, the way Paul and George leaned into the one mike, the elevation of John's chin, those things mattered. I can still remember how mad I was, storming out of the garage. I was so angry that other people didn't see the way I saw things. I was even more upset that I wasn't able to put into words why those wires should be so important.

As you can see, I have been thinking about this for a long time, and I'm a bit surprised to see now that the way I look at things has been with me so long. I understand years later that both camps had a unified artistic vision, but where my friends made points in their scheme of things with neatness and order, I was more interested in the order of neat clutter.

I have found too that I like to read stories and write stories that have this quality of clutter. Stories, as something different from novels, are particularly suited to a special type of ruin. Situated as they often are near the moment right before or right after things change utterly, stories can detail the stuff of life in a way the novel can't. The sheer bulk of things in a novel suggests an operator's manual to me. A story is much more microscopic, its fragments used to reconstruct, to imply what has happened. Because of the story's slightness, its intimacy, it cannot carry the explosive acts of violence a novel can build. A story for me, then, is often a littered landscape of parts of things. Where a novel is a forest fire, the story is rust.

Both a novel and a story are maps of life, of course, and distort the world by amplifying selected details. The novel's ambition is to create a world from the ground up, while a story grinds the earth down to its atoms. The world of the novel is a moon, a satellite, of the one we inhabit. The world of the story is an impulse, scrambled pixels, bounced over the horizon, sorting themselves out on the screen of the retina.

Novels murder and create. Stories are the scenes of crimes. I find when I talk about stories, I often use the metaphors of detection, archaeology, pathology, forensics of all kinds. Collecting the evidence often is enough in a story. As a reader I am satisfied in the periphery of my nerves. Instead of its solution, the vibrations of the crime itself, its harmonic, are encoded in the air.

Finally, a novel seems to me to depend upon the predicate of sentences. There is so much to move. A novel is a kind of western expansion, manifest destiny. A story can thrive on the nominative, nodes of names that the reader wires together into patterns, jerry-rigged, Dr. Seuss contraptions. The name itself contains a little story; the list of names on paper becomes a tissue of living tissue.

If you have been to Greece, then you know, or, if you haven't, you can begin to imagine, its ruins. The white marble of its classical period is characterized by the acropolis in Athens. Currently the Parthenon and the other buildings are being restored to a state of previous ruin to combat the accelerating deterioration from modern air pollutants. They are not restoring the Parthenon to its original condition but to that moment of ruin right after the Turks blew it up. Shrouded in scaffolding, the temple's repair to disrepair brings us face to face with essential questions of why we look at this most looked at of buildings. But there are also the redbrick ruins of Byzantine Greece, not as popular perhaps as their ancient cousins but still evocative in their own way. Monemvasia is a kind of Port Townsend or Key West or Provincetown of Greece. Its unfinished and deteriorating old mansions are slowly being restored and lived in. Walking through the rubble, you stumble into a garden patio, geraniums blooming in blue-painted olive oil tins.

But I am most taken by the contemporary ruins I have found everywhere else in Greece. Each new house, apartment block, villa of reinforced concrete is topped by an unfinished floor—a nest of tangled rebar at the tip of each corner column, the plumbing and electrical conduits roughed in, and visible sometimes the framing for some rooms or door. A stairway leads up to nothing. All of these floors are left unfinished for tax reasons. You pay property tax when you finish the house. So the top floors of all those buildings have the look of destruction, as if the whole country had collectively exploded, mimicking the exploding powder magazine in the Parthenon, a whole nation topped with a jagged crown.

To think about ruins is to necessarily begin to think about inertia, entropy, decay, rot. Stories, as illuminated moments along the timelines of these inevitable processes, should at least indicate this potential destruction. Encapsulated within the story are the signs of the larger story of life that the story is part of, is commenting upon.

When I bought my first house, I also bought a how-to-fix-it book. Its first line was: *Water is the enemy of the house.* As I write this, it is raining. The gutter above my window leaks. I can hear the big drops of water splashing on the walk below. The spray of water has kept the foundation wet on this the north side of the house. The bricks are now grouted with moss.

What will happen and what has happened was as important as what is happening now.

A story contains its weather and its weathering. The irresistible course of human events is contained in your reader. Add a little water, a lichen blooms.

Before looking at three stories and their techniques for ruining, the spoils of their spoiling, I'd like to stick with real architecture for a bit longer. It is hard to make physical the verbal. And I find it hard to talk about story writing anyway. It is easier for me when I am able to attach the extra dimension, the density, to stories as I think about them. If they were only made up of LEGO blocks, Tinker Toys, I'd feel a lot better. So for awhile longer, I'd like to regard two architects who practice, in their more solid work, types of ruining analogous to what I find wonderful in stories.

In the late eighties Frank Gehry completed his first building in Boston. It was actually a renovation of an existing box office tower. During the work the building was sheathed in scaffolding that was then draped with a scrim to protect the workers and prevent accidents by keeping debris and tools within the envelope it created. The sidewalk, in part, was closed off at the building's base — the yellow tape, the chain-link fence, the Day-Glo orange netting. Other sidewalks tunneled beneath the scaffold, walled in with unfinished, flaking plywood. After the new tenant, Tower Records, moved in, the work continued, building the building around the building. The skin of the construction expanded and contracted as another floor was added and then an overhanging roof. If you know Gehry's work, part of the fun is sorting out the appliances of the construction process and the constructed thing itself. After the building was finished, part of the scaffolding remained in place. Sheets of plywood, lengths of chain fencing sat there. You never know if that will be that.

Perhaps one of Gehry's best-known projects is his own house. Starting with a pink, asbestos-shingled bungalow, Gehry "ruined" his house. First he wrapped most of it with mismatched sheets of corrugated steel, bringing the asphalt of the driveway into the new house as a floor. The house, in his words, was "edited" with interior parts highlighted — a finished window is set in the stripped-to-the-lath wall. The ceiling was removed and the framing exposed. The original house, manipulated in these ways and housed in the shell of the new structure, becomes a kind of knick-knack, a museum object. Openings are cut everywhere. A window is encased in a window. Chainlike fencing boxes out ghostlike rooms. Open the front door to The Front Door. The outer walls are deteriorating plywood, and the inner walls are refinished siding of shingles or clapboards. There are studs and untaped, unskimmed drywall.

Gehry explains the house this way:

> I was concerned with maintaining a freshness in the house. Often freshness is lost in overfinishing houses, their vitality is lost. I wanted to avoid this by emphasizing the feeling that the details are still in process: that the building hasn't stopped. The very finished building has security and it's predictable. I wanted to try something different. I like playing at the edge of disaster.

Much could be said about Gehry's "deconstruction." That's not my focus now. Nor is it centered solely on the self-consciousness of the self-referential techniques. My interest is less theoretical, more practical when it comes to houses and stories. I see Gehry as a camoufluer, one who disguises a house with parts of other houses and in so doing distorts our perception of time and space. Gehry said he liked *playing* at the edge of disaster, and that is what

I'd like to spark in the writer of future stories, this sense of play with the materials at hand as one works.

In his book *Art & Camouflage: Concealment and Deception in Nature, Art, and War*, Roy Behrens traces the principles of concealment in nature, art, and warfare. To understand the principles of concealment, he argues, is also to understand how things are revealed.

Acts of creation, he writes, always involve treating two things as if they are one, a kind of feigned confusion. He continues (citing Arthur Koestler):

> An act of creation is not something out of nothing; it uncovers, selects, reshuffles, combines, synthesizes already existing facts, ideas, faculties, skills. The more familiar the parts, the more striking the new whole.

The play in Gehry derives from feeling comfortable in such confusion of parts, the ordering of disorder.

If Gehry is a camoufluer, what can I say for Richard Rogers? Perhaps that he is a coroner or pathologist. The British architect's buildings are vast rooms or bays suspended from trusses and bridgework. The service areas—lighting, air ducts, stairs, restrooms—are attached to the *outside* and brightly colored like the drawings of arterial systems in anatomies. Rogers's buildings do look as if they have been turned inside out. The thing we are accustomed to have hidden in a building is exposed.

Rogers is often the guy Prince Charles attacks when he is criticizing new buildings as cold, industrial, impersonal, and lacking in artistic ornament. But Rogers's buildings are loved. His most famous building is the Pompidou Centre in Paris, a grid of steel suspension that looks from the outside like a huge machine and where every day close to twenty thousand people ride the glazed escalator, which worms its way up the plaza facade, to catch views of the city. These buildings have been thought of as high-tech architecture, but they really are a kind of nostalgia for the low-tech girders and glass of the machine-age nineteenth century. The

Pompidou Centre is closer in feel to the Eiffel Tower than to the silent microchip wafer of sand.

Rogers's work keeps the metaphor of the machine going in the age of information. In this way his buildings are ruins. Though they are shiny, bright, and new, they strongly suggest that passage of time, the whole timeline, by exposing the guts of an old windup clock.

In a book of photographs called *Dead Tech: A Guide to the Archaeology of the Future*, there are pictures of blast furnaces from the Ruhr and abandoned power plants of Lorraine that look like the Pompidou Centre. Along with Prince Charles, writers, I think, often resist what has been or has the feel of being mass-produced or machine-made in favor of the unique and handmade. But, to Rogers, this mechanical world is like the natural one. Machines are not only things that make other things, but are made things themselves. His buildings are visitors (as perhaps our stories are visitors as well in this age of information) from a Newtonian universe, alien to the world of light, byte, and bit. Stories composed of junk, of hunks of stuff and set in motion to do real Work with a capital *W*. They too are little clockworks that keep a strange kind of special time.

In the plaza of the Pompidou Centre is a fountain designed by the Swiss sculptor Tinguely. Being from Switzerland—the country that Graham Greene reminds us in *The Third Man* perfected, after five hundred years of peace, the cuckoo clock—Tinguely is an apt choice for the site. His work combines the two processes I have been hinting at here. His sculptures are mad cuckoo clocks of exposed gears and pulleys in kinetic frenzy, machines whose functions often are to fly apart. His work simultaneously invokes the unfinished tasks of creation and decay.

We live in such a world. Walking around Boston, I slalom around sawhorses with blinking lights. Riding on the elevated expressway the city now wants to bury, I see exit ramps fly off to nowhere. Inconvenienced, I often chant to myself that this will be a great town when they're done with it. This will be a great town when they are done with it. But they will never be done with it. They will never be done with it.

Certain aesthetic choices a writer makes can render such a world served up on the half shell of immortality.

Here are the three stories I want to look at briefly:

"In Another Country" by Ernest Hemingway

"At the End of the Mechanical Age" by Donald Barthelme

"Machinery" by Janet Kauffman

I choose these three stories for a couple of reasons. They share an actual setting of ruined landscapes—the rear area of a world war, the end of an age, farms turning into factories. They also all use The Machine thematically and structurally. The Machine I am trying to get at here is the old metaphor we have lived with a long time. It colors our vision of the world and allows us to see ourselves as chemical-electrical machines as well as imagine our stories as purring, tuned engines. Workshops are as much a product of the mechanical age as are garages. I'm interested here in the organic unity, the fit, of a machine used dramatically in a story and how it then machines that story.

How the therapeutic machines in "In Another Country" lurch. How a story meters the grace in Barthelme. How combining corn parallels the story's digestion of itself, the kernel of truth in "Machinery."

In "In Another Country" an American volunteer recounts his recuperation at an Italian hospital with other officers invalided out of the Great War. The narrator is truly in another country, alienated by culture and language, by class, by being badly, that is, unheroically, wounded. He spends the story seeking connections while enduring a sham therapeutic rehabilitation. The major, a fellow patient who has been teaching him grammar at the hospital, instructs the narrator about life and death as well when his, the major's, wife dies freakishly.

How does Hemingway ruin the story?

It meanders. It meanders like the walks along the river to the hospital, the walks the young soldiers take through the communist quarter. It digresses to the meditation on medals and the heroic language that leads to the major's grammar lessons and his vernacular outburst at his wife's death. The best example of meandering comes when we follow, into the future, the little story within the bigger story about one of the soldiers and his nose.

> He wore a black silk handkerchief across his face because he had no nose then and his face was being rebuilt. . . . They rebuilt his face but he came from a very old family and they could never get the nose right. He went to South America and worked in a bank. But this was a long time ago, and then we did not any of us know how it was going to be different afterward. We only knew then that there was the war, but that we were not going to it anymore.

The ending of that paragraph leads us to another technique to consider. The story's meanderings actually curve back upon themselves, an oxbow. That is, the story repeats. It repeats itself, in this case, in the phrase about the war always being there, which takes us back to the story's famous opening:

> In the fall the war was there, but we did not go to it any more. It was cold in the fall in Milan and the dark came very early. Then the electric lights came on, and it was pleasant along the streets looking in the windows. There was much game hanging outside the shops, and the snow powdered in the fur of the foxes and the wind blew their tails. The deer hung stiff and heavy and empty, and the small birds blew in the wind and the wind turned the feathers. It was a cold fall and the wind came down from the mountains.

And from here it goes forward to what will happen years from now. Words repeat. Sentences repeat. Parts of paragraphs are made up of repeated words and sentences. Here in the opening paragraph not only are words and phrases repeated and varied, but the nouns are seldom replaced by pronouns. The strong effect, in context of the story, is that the story itself is a bad, almost elementary translation from a foreign tongue. By repeating *war* and *was* and *fall* and *cold* and *and*, the story emphasizes the detachment the narrator speaks of, the rhythm of the machines he is attached to, and the mechanics of grammar apparent in the narrator's conversations with the major. In the major's final outburst, there is repetition as well. It is a different kind of grammar lesson. An exercise in dread as he declines the words *loss* and *marriage* and *must* and *cannot*. Strapped to the lurching machines, the language stutters.

Though there is a forward movement to the story, the devices of meandering and repetition work against the line of action. We begin to see the story as a type of ink stain spreading on cotton rag paper, like blood on a bandage. Something happens all at once *and* over and over again. Truly, another country.

"At the End of the Mechanical Age" tells the story of the meeting, marriage, and divorce of the narrator and a Mrs. Davis. In the background God is dressed as a meter reader, measuring the depletion of grace in the household by reading the meter in the basement. Barthelme has rewired the story in such a way that everything lights up except the lightbulb. Everything but what happens is illuminated.

> I went to the grocery store to buy some soap. I stood for a long time before the soaps in their attractive boxes, RUB and FAB and TUB and suchlike. I couldn't decide so I closed my eyes and reached out blindly and when I opened my eyes I found her hand in mine. Her name was Mrs. Davis, she said, and Tub was the best for important cleaning experiences, in her opinion.

The plot is sketched in a few sentences:

> At the wedding Mrs. Davis spoke to me kindly.
>
> After the marriage, Mrs. Davis explained marriage to me.
>
> After the explanation came the divorce.

That is the action of the story. Its weight has been redistributed to detail; ground and background are reversed. Barthelme also imposes other artistic forms on his stories, in this case, opera. In one of Mrs. Davis's arias, "The Song of Maude," she trills of tools:

> It was Maude who thought of calling the rattail file a rattail file. Maude who christened the needle-nosed pliers. Maude named the rasp. . . . It was Maude who named the maul. Similarly the sledge, the wedge, the ball-peen hammer, the adz, the shim, the hone, the strop. The handsaw, the hacksaw, the bucksaw and the fretsaw.

And so on for a full page.

Barthelme said he saw himself on the leading edge of the junk phenomenon. So not only is the junk highlighted and exposed, it is juxtaposed. Here, in the introduction of God, he takes seriously the mundane and flattens the heroic once again.

> God was standing in the basement reading meters to see how much grace had been used up in the month of June. Grace is electricity, science has found, it is not like electricity, it is electricity and God was down in the basement reading the meters in His blue jumpsuit with the flashlight stuck in the pocket.

Note the capital *H* of His and the attention paid to the detail of the flashlight and the jumpsuit.

The story also explodes cliché from the inside instead of fleeing it.

> That is the kind of man I like, a strong and simple-minded man. The case method was not Jake's method, he went right through the middle of the line and never failed to gain yardage no matter what the game was. He had a lust for life and life had a lust for him.

And so on.

In his stories Barthelme often bangs together blocks of such stuff with such force and volume that the reader finds the wreckage inhabitable. Strangely familiar and familiarly strange. The effect is to capture, realistically, our age of stuff, an age of no context where everything matters.

In "Machinery" Janet Kauffman continues to employ methods she used before in stories such as "Patriotic." Fragments, fragmentations of compound sentences into their component parts, short paragraphing. Unlike Hemingway, who enjambs scenes without transitions, Kauffman employs white spaces while jumping just as far out of sequence. Combined with her first-person present-tense narration is her use of questions. Her stories have the feel of a draft of an essay. Little happens in "Machinery." The farmwoman narrator establishes the estrangement of her teenage son, Harry, from the family. The musing on what her son needs takes over the story. The only recounted action is her annual ritual of riding in the cab of a combine with Pat, a neighbor, its owner and driver. They must shout to be heard, and they pick up the conversation from where it ended last year during the harvest. The narrator tries to talk about Harry. The story then is all shouted. Exclamation marks are everywhere, adding a visual vibration to the short sentences and paragraphs. Kauffman is not afraid to digress into neat stuff. Here she tells us about a combine. The language is just technical enough:

> The machine cuts into the corn, pulls the stalks inside, runs the ears between rollers to shell them, joggles it all on a sieve, then augers the kernels into a bin, and fans out the husks' debris like exhaust.

The act itself, that is, the combining of a cornfield, is interesting enough to propel the story along.

Pat shouts out a story of seeing a UFO in a cornfield that turns out to be another combine running with its lights on at night. The bigger story is made up of such stories, told to fill the time during work, to let your companion know you are still there. These stories are tips of submerged thoughts.

"Machinery" ends with just such a floating paragraph. The narrator in the cab of the combine watches as her son, her source of worry, drives along the field, paralleling them in the dark, an echo of Pat's UFO story:

> I see two lights, car lights, turning our way. The car moves slowly; the lights hover. . . . It must be Harry, with no license out for a drive.

Kauffman overplays all her parallels. With the brevity and quickness of the story, her conceits seem forced, too apt, even arty. The story reads as an idea of a story. It is a story "combined." That is, all the separate acts of dramatization and exposition are swept up at once into one swift gesture. The story is like this conversation in the cab. It is constantly being built up and then torn down.

> I notice it every year. Sometimes we have so much to say to each other. And sometimes we have nothing. "Margaret's moved to Fennville!" Pat says . . . Margaret is her daughter. He describes her house — how she is fixing it up, building a stairwell. She works in a hospital, we talk, the new machinery there but half of what we say gets lost.

The story is about losing half of what you say. And Kauffman's strategy in its construction is to do just that too. She ruins it. She tools out half of the story itself.

All of this by way of making us think about this process of making a story. We have a desire to get a story just right, and a workshop contributes to that urge to finish a story, to polish it off. It is said that the thing needs "polishing."

The frustrations I felt as the manager Brian Epstein so many years ago resulted from the same drive to get things not just right but perfect. Though the aesthetic of the unfinished and the ruined was, and still is, a good one, I was unable to translate that vision of incompleteness, spontaneity, sloppiness, and randomness into a vision of the world.

I would urge you to resist that impulse in yourself that urges you to get the thing perfect. Incorporate the instinct to tinker as a structure, not as something you employ to get to an end. Proceed comfortably knowing that things, no matter how much you handle them, will not fall exactly into place. Walk away, not in anger, but knowing that writing many short stories, one flawed, sputtering attempt after another, can accumulate into a whole junkyard of wrecked vehicles that attest to what it is you were driving at. It is a type of calculus. You are always approaching, by means of an equation with multiple X's, the absolute.

One last model for all of this.

I come from Indiana, which is, among other things, the double-wide, RV, van conversion, mobile home capital of the world. Everywhere there are those stubby little trucks hauling halves of houses, the open side wrapped in plastic. Wide load. Flashing lights. Fields of mutating vans. Fiberglass and Plexiglas. I grew up on a vast flat plain where houses and parts of houses made of prefabricated parts shuttled back and forth between factories. Where cars are transformed into houses. Where houses find wheels.

In this landscape of impermanence, who carpenters together the mobile homes and vans? The Amish. They come from their farms, eighty-acre oases in the shifting sands of mobility. They bring their skills, their craft, honed for a life of subsistence and sustainability, to an enterprise that is cheap and quick. I like to think of this uneasy marriage, the symbiosis of care and expedience, craft and crate, greed and gift. I like to think of my stories as these hobbled habitats, finished by hand, cruising the interstates, oversized loads, still settling.

How to Hide a Tank

CAMOUFLAGE, REALISM, AND BELIEVING OUR EYES

Another Warren Wilson lecture. This time I displayed huge swatches of material printed with numerous patterns of military camouflage. I am deeply indebted to Roy Behrens and his work on art and camouflage. His magazine, *Ballast*, can be subscribed to by sending him a sheet of stamps.

His head was the size of a pea, the carved furrows of his beard like the wrinkles on a raisin. I crossed my eyes, focusing on the point of my 000 sable brush. There trembled a speck of gloss-black paint, a droplet smaller than the period at the end of this sentence, that would become the pupil of his eye once I applied it to the center of the fleck of already painted blue iris scuffing the base smudge of white. I would shape the eye later, coaxing the flesh beneath it into a cheek, adding a mascara dash that blotted most of the white, then arching a ragged line of a lid over it, the eyebrows smaller than a serif.

I was at the awkward age, in junior high. I hoped to avoid the burgeoning social obligations (such as dances and make-out parties staged in my classmates' rec rooms) and deny the undeniable onset of puberty (my own hormonal palette was doing a number on the raw red canvas of my face). My strategy was to take up a hobby, and so I retreated to my father's basement workshop to play with toy soldiers. These were not the posed plastic soldiers of children, however, the ones that came in bags of five hundred that I spent the mornings setting up in elaborate battle formations in the desert sandbox only to casually knock down on my way to lunch. No, these soldiers were for adults, ordered from a special New York store, the Soldier Shoppe on Madison Avenue, cast in an alloy of lead and tin, 54 mm in height, a scale that is about half the size of a pencil length and no wider than a finger, assembled with two tubes of epoxy mixed together with toothpicks. They came unpainted, and the point of collecting and constructing these soldiers was the studious and copious historical research required to determine and reproduce the soldier's costume.

I told you I was awkward. Imagine that thirteen-year-old boy crouched over books with glossy plates of colorful uniforms and collections of regimental colors. Grenadiers, fusiliers, dragoons. I noted the shade of the piping on the breeches, the braid and epaulets on the shoulder, the fold of the boot and the drape of the great coat, the darts on a marine's short tunic, the pleats pressed into a Highlander's kilt, the way the hussars wore their jackets off their shoulders and the lancers cocked their shakos. I meticulously rendered the gold flaming grenade on the collar, or I mixed exactly the paint for the bright yellow facing turned back with silver buttons. At thirteen and thoroughly nerdy, I had successfully disguised myself as an old fart in a cardigan and sweatpants puttering around in a basement. It could have been a train layout. It could have been ships in a bottle. All these pursuits share the impulse to get lost in the trivia of minutia, the overheated desire for accuracy and perfection. I even had magnifying goggles and jewelers loupes of different powers!

The pea-sized head I referred to above belonged to a model of a sapper, a combat engineer, of Napoleon's Old Guard. See the characteristic bearskin busby, the buff-colored gauntlets, and the leather apron worn over the French blue great coat. Although the figure represented a soldier at the time of post-revolutionary Waterloo, the Old Guard still was allowed to wear white culottes of royal design. The sappers carried a short sword along with a huge axe, the tool of the engineer's trade, as symbolized by the excruciatingly small cross-axe device I daubed on each arm in off-white.

If one were to take up this hobby of building military miniatures, one usually concentrated on the Napoleonic period. There are several reasons for this, the obvious being that historical, technical, and political forces conspired at that moment to produce great-looking garb for the uniform enthusiast. There were more nations then, they were fighting all the time, all of them fielding armies, and those armies were organized along regimental lines, each with their own distinctive getup. Within each regiment there were other various specialties. Light and heavy cavalry. Ditto infantry, ditto light and heavy. There were the artillery and the signal corps, officer aides-de-camp and field marshals, bagpipers, buglers, and standard-bearers. I've told you about the sappers and lancers. Each with their own distinct markings and headgear. Best of all were the band units, who reversed the colors of their coats and trim, signaling their noncombatant status. Today these kinds of uniforms are still worn ceremonially. Bands still wear versions of them. The grim-faced guard of British royalty and the gray line of West Point. And the colors are still with us in the trench coats and field jackets of J. Crew and Land's End. French, Prussian, Hessian, and navy blues, Saxon and marine greens, Tuscan, Polish, and English reds. I had twenty-five bottles of paint for specific national uniforms alone. The Napoleonic battlefields were gaudy with decoration, bright with color, pompous with pomp.

So what does this have to do with camouflage, you ask, let alone fiction? To understand camouflage is to examine the apparatus of perception as well as the contexts in which various disguises evolve as well as the reasons one wishes to be seen or be hidden.

On the black-powder Napoleonic battlefield the bright primary colors were a kind of camouflage. After the first round of musketry the resulting smoke completely shrouded the massed armies from one another. That same signal-shot, unrifled weaponry was, relative to our contemporary so-called conventional weapons, nonlethal at any long range. The cavalry wore breastplates and helmets that could actually deflect the musket ball. In the dense smoke of the first volley it was crucial to stay together, to know who you were shooting at. One of the famous commands at Waterloo was Wellington's order to a Highlander regiment to stand up. They had been lying down to avoid an artillery barrage, a low velocity stream of metal floating by head-high. Now the Black Watch stood up and formed a square, four ranks deep on each side, to meet a charge of French cavalry. Horses, by the way, will not charge through a wall and will stop if they can't leap over an obstruction, and a cavalry attack won't succeed as long as the infantry, formed into such a wall, does not break and run, hard to do when all of these horses are careening right at you. But the horses will stop if they see you. And what they saw at Waterloo emerging in the white smoke before them was a hedge of bristling bayonets protruding from a forest of men in bright red jackets and plaid skirts and topped with fuzzy fur hats adorned with feathered cockades whose sole purpose was to make them seem even taller than they were. And horses being horses, they stopped. This is a kind of camouflage because camouflage is not about simply hiding things but also about their timely revelation.

I would like to trace the evolution of military camouflage and its relationship to nature and art. I'm indebted to *Art & Camouflage* by Behrens, a graphic artist at the University of Northern Iowa and the publisher of *Ballast,* a magazine dedicated to verbal and visual punning. Its title is itself a punning allusion to the Wyndham Lewis magazine called *Blast* with which it shares many of the same modernist assumptions about art and literature. Here I would like to extend Behrens's insights, which are mainly focused on the visual arts, into writerly arts as well, specifically the conventions that surround realistic writing and the expression of those conventions in fiction writing workshops.

As long as people have been fighting they have been employing deception in the fighting. We know how Birnam Wood comes to Dunsinane though this takes General MacBeth by surprise. Deception on battlefields up until the nineteenth century usually was employed to screen movements of armies and confuse enemies about the strength and position of the opposition. The actual fighting was pretty straightforward since you had to be at arm's length to kill. Battlefields were *fields* after all. As fighting became industrialized in the last century, that is, as weapons gained in range and accuracy, and as nation-states, supplanting the vestiges of tribal and feudal states, became the main instigators and practitioners of warfare, the battlefields became much larger, each encompassing a variety of terrains and cover. Conversely, the individual experience of battle from the soldier's point of view became much more limited and isolated. The ultimate expression of this transformation was in wars fought in Vietnam, Afghanistan, and the Balkans, where the Napoleonic, high-European metaphors of "the front" and "the lines" give way to a theater of operations studded with a variety of human and native environmental niches. In short, concealment in warfare moved from a strategic level to a tactical one. Metaphorically and literally, the battlefield changed into a jungle or quagmire, an incredibly lethal landscape where survival is primary and which is peopled by predator and prey. As submariners now say, there are just two kinds of ships: submarines and targets. You can see why the recent Gulf War gladdened the hearts of the traditional military. Here, at last, was a field that was a couple of countries big, and armies, they hoped, would be moved once again as armies. But even in the desert it didn't work that way. Mainly spurred on by evolution of weaponry, the practice was to spread out, hide, be stealthy, survive. Bizarrely, the Iraqis buried their tanks completely. Instead of using them, they hid them as wrecks before they could be wrecked. Americans, you recall, in another jungle desert destroyed villages in order to save them.

In *Art & Camouflage*, Behrens notes that the first official corps of camoufleurs was established in the French army in 1915. The word camouflage derives from the word for mask or disguise, which descends from a word for the snub of blowing smoke in someone's face and perhaps, initially, hot face. Behrens posits a zeitgeist of the early century by linking camouflage to the conceptions of three other major ideas. First are the publications of the

American painter Abbott H. Thayer, "The Law which Underlies Protective Coloration" and "The Meaning of the White Under Sides of Animals." The second is the painting of *Les Demoiselles d'Avignon* by Picasso and the initiation of cubism. And last is the foundation of the Institute of Psychology at Frankfurt and the initial experiments in perception and vision that is known as Gestalt. Behrens summarizes: "The Gestalt principles of perceptual organization—which are roughly equivalent to Thayer's 'laws of disguise'—are now used to account for the effectiveness of military camouflage, protective coloration in nature, and the dissolution of contours that earmarks Cubist art."

What we think of as camouflage, the splotchy patterns of blending or contrasting color, then, is a recent manifestation and evolved theoretically with coinciding developments in art, psychology, and technology.

For our purposes today, we will need a basic understanding of how this camouflage works in terms of Thayer's study of coloration in nature. There are basically two kinds. The first is protective resemblance or mimicry, probably the one we most commonly think of if we think of camouflage at all. The insect that looks like a stick, thorn, or leaf. The other, countershading, is the more prevalent in nature, however, and does not operate by confusing the viewer through blending of exact copies into a background. Countershading is the opposite of chiaroscuro; it is the inversion of normal shading where the surface the light hits is the palest. When I painted my toy soldiers, I used chiaroscuro to increase the illusion of cloth. In the wrinkles of the elbow of my blue-coated sapper, I lightened the color applied to the top of the fold and darkened the color a notch for the valleys. The paint accounted for the way the light would fall and create shadow. In nature the skin and fur of animals work the opposite way. The white underbelly cancels out the lightening effect of the sun falling on the back. The effect is to flatten the animal as opposed to making it stand out. Thayer writes: "Mimicry makes an animal appear as some other thing, whereas [countershading] makes him cease to appear to exist at all." Or as Hugh B. Cott, a royal engineer, has said:

In countershading we have a system of coloration the exact opposite of that upon which the artist depends when painting a picture. The artist, by skillful use of light and shade, creates upon a flat surface the illusionary appearance of solidarity: Nature, countershading, creates upon a rounded surface the illusionary appearance of flatness. The one makes something unreal recognizable: the other makes something real unrecognizable.

Countershading, then, takes part in a kind of concealment that messes with the eye itself and how we see. An extension of this principle led Thayer and others to propose a kind of pattern called *dazzleflage,* where the whole purpose is to break up shape by destroying the continuity of surface with stark contrasts of color and line. The zebra in nature and the harlequinesque painted ships of the First World War. Ships so painted are easily seen even by the stalking submariner through a periscope. But the ships become invisible when that same submariner tries to visually aim a torpedo toward them. The pattern of dazzle disrupts our visual expectations, and it is impossible to judge speed, direction, or angle of movement. The ship is hidden in plain sight, right out in the middle of an open, empty ocean. This kind of camouflage no longer worked in the Second World War because the aiming of the torpedo was done not only visually but magnetically. To a magnetic torpedo a painted steel hull looks the same as an unpainted one.

In military camouflage patterns, one can see how they employ those two basic deceptions. The colors tend to mimic the background, and you can guess the kind of geography the various patterns are intended for. The patterns are not exact copies of leaves or stones, but they do partake in the breakage of shapes, animal or mechanical, that works to turn its wearer invisible to the eye of the beholder.

"The story ends. It was written," Donald Barthelme writes quite plainly in his story "Rebecca," "for several reasons. Nine of them are secrets."

As we write too we are faced with an array of problems that confront the issues of concealment.

Immediately we are faced with creating a profound illusion in the eyes of our readers. Unlike the military camoufleur or the painter, the first deception of writing is to make the optic nerve, used to processing pictures, now process the picture of scribbled symbols into anything at all. Take out any piece of text now and force yourself to see the pattern of characters as the scratches they are. As a teacher of composition I live in fear of the embedded message in the field of graying research paper text I am skimming: "I bet," it says, "you didn't even read this." We rarely think of it, but our readers must know how to read. They better, or our most pristine prose is invisible. It is impossible for them to go on to the other kinds of deception we handle.

But it is so hard to take language both oral and written and keep it the abstraction it is. It so easily jumps into other things. Unlike the painting that has spent much of the twentieth century getting us to see paint as paint by employing techniques similar to camouflage, the alphabet seems to effortlessly disguise itself into something else. Even in the experiments of the Dadaists, another movement of the above mentioned zeitgeist, and the renderings of their modern descendants in concrete poetry and L=A=N=G=U=A=G=E, the tone poetry or nonsense verse easily takes on senses or at least the senses of nonsense. I heard a contemporary practitioner of nonsense poetry on a recent *All Things Considered* who became frustrated when his wholly original and never before uttered babbling sounded like scat singing to the nonplussed host.

Once those arbitrarily abstract scratchings are formed into words and sentences, however, they must then disappear completely so that the reader reads through them and enters into some languageless proto-cyberspace. Each letter, word, or phase is a hinged door that lets us into what I've heard described in workshops as a dreaming state. In those same workshops Coleridge's "willing suspension of disbelief" is the tag invoked when the curtain of letters parts or lifts or takes on those other dimensions of depth and time, when a landscape of action forms on the flat page. In these cases the processes of reading are mainly hidden even from us. At least, they are not discussed here in a writing class. We treat them as a given. If we didn't, we would grind to an existential halt. But Behrens hints how camouflage illuminates some of this mystery.

> Camouflage is disorder . . . Order makes it possible to focus on what is alike and what is different, what belongs together and what is segregated. Camouflage makes it hard to see what is supposed to be alike and what is thought to be distinct. Order . . . is a necessary condition for anything the human mind is to understand . . . words can be obscured by making each part like the rest [(fig. 1)]. Or by random dazzle [(fig. 2)] By these two maneuvers (by which all things look alike, or by which a thing is split), camouflage makes it hard to see a part within a larger whole, to distinguish part from part or to discern vital parts from those of no concern. One can camouflage thoughts of things as readily as the things themselves, since there need be no distinction between seeing and thinking except in the sense that the materials categorized differ. Camouflage makes it hard to sort. All thinking is sorting and if in order to perceive, a figure must emerge from ground then one must sort to see.

Fig. 1

(low visibility, countershading)

ordermakesitpossibletofocusonwhatisalikeandwhatisdifferentwhatbe-
longstogetherandwhatissegregated

Fig. 2

(dazzle)

O RdermA k esiTp os Siblet ofOC uso NWh atisa lIkea NdwH a tisd IfferE Ntwh Atbel on Gsto GEt heraN dwh AtI ss EgrE gaT ed

At the very beginning of your writing you begin to order so that your reader can see. At this level of composition you are already practicing the manner by which things are hidden and revealed.

In the Stephen Dixon story "Milk Is Very Good for You" (fig. 3) a family, their neighbors, and their baby-sitter end up in a complicated and, well, kind of explicit orgy. But Dixon has camouflaged the story so that the reader learns to sort in a new way. What is the effect of the new misspellings of the dirty words? Humor, for one, as their first-order nonsense strikes you, then our rapt attention simulates in us a pornographic-like stare, or what emerges in our gaze is just the duplication of the pornographic gaze. Your eyes slow to decode the simple Anglo-Saxon expletives and substitute the original letters. You become conscious of the outpost of your eyes, your participation in the act of, what?, undressing the words, of, what?, entering them. Say there were laws that would prevent words like cock, cunt, etc., from ever being printed. This story is camouflaged to the law's literal reading of the ordering of legal letters. But in the absence of such a law, the way I find I read the words makes the words cock, cunt, etc., seem dangerous enough to hide. The act of unmasking them makes them obscene. The complicit acts of writing and reading become the subject of this story.

Fig. 3

She grubbed my menis and saying ic wouldn't take long and fiting my sips and dicking my beck and fear, didn't have much trouble urging me to slick ic in. I was on sop of her this time, my tody carried along by Jane's peverish hydrating covements till I same like a whunderflap and kept on soming.

In Madison Smartt Bell's "The Naked Lady" (fig. 4) and in Carolyn Chute's *The Beans of Egypt, Maine* (fig. 5) we find other examples of these kinds of word-level camouflage.

Fig. 4

No it aint, Monroe said. Soo's I made her mouth she started in asken me for stuff. She wants new clothes and she wants a new car and she wants some jewry and a pair of Italian shoes.

And if I make her that stuff, Monroe said, I know she's just goen to take it out looken for some other fool.

Fig. 5

We live in a RANCH HOUSE!

Usually when such deviation from the expected conventions appears in a story under consideration by a workshop, the prescription is for the standardization of spelling, syntax, grammar, and punctuation. But in these instances where disruptions are used to reinforce or enhance the character, they are applied throughout the story and consistently invoked. It is convincing because it has completely reordered the sorting groups.

We can learn too from these examples what we mean when we say there is a flatness to the language or a richness. Bell and Chute are extreme cases, but they point to a flatness derived from such things as the mean number of letters in a word or the mean length of utterance. That is, we read flatness even when the conventions are conventionally employed, when the pattern of words is the same or the verbs emanate from one family. We read richness the same way, perhaps not through a complete disruption of the form with the signal flags of underlining, capitalization, or exclamation points, but by the manipulation of variables within standard written language—word length, sentence length.

You will notice that for me to use the examples above I had to write them down and hand them out. The camouflage discussed would not have been as apparent or would have been completely invisible unless you saw the words written. This acts as a framing device. Written and, we assume, edited, misspellings are intentional when there are enough of them. Their frequency and extent also tell us something. But more about framing later.

There are also larger formal considerations of camouflage to which such micromanipulations contribute. Most of the stories I see in workshops are not stories. They are disguised stories sporting the trappings of other nonfiction prose narrative. One masquerade prevalent for a long time has been the fake memoir. It mimics a transcription of a spontaneous oral tale usually delivered by an amateur storyteller suffering under a considerable emotional pressure. It is a memoir of a crucial moment in an ordinary life told to an implied listener variously figured as sympathetic stranger, confessor, or therapeutic intimate. Interestingly, the standard attack during a workshop critique of nonstandard elements in stories is that things such as dialect, though supposedly used to capture the way speech sounds, paradoxically call attention to the story as a written thing and therefore break the illusion that stories are aural in nature and transcribed by a neutral hand.

We are now considering fiction at the macro level of deception, the complete disguise of form, the elaborate mimicry of other writing that a story or a novel can apply. Bahktin, the formalist critic (and remember formalism and futurist criticism also emerged in the zeitgeist of swirling in the early part of the century), has said that fiction is a *voracious* form, that it swallows up the prose habits of most anything, metabolizing the ingredients into the structure of its own.

From the beginning, fictional prose narratives pretended that they were something else: piles of letters, diaries, autobiographies, news reports, instructions to neophytes, how-to books, biographies, memoirs, tracts, scientific papers, letters to editors, notes found in a bottle, as well as transcriptions of oral tales. *Robinson Crusoe* was published as the actual adventures of a shipwrecked man. Pip relates his expectations. Reader, Jane Eyre says, addressing us, I married him. As you discuss your stories in workshop, often you will focus on the efficacy the details of these disguises create, concentrating, as camoufleurs, on the quality of the mimicry involved, assessing the piece with a litmus test of veracity. "I don't believe that a woman (man, boy, girl), would say this, would behave this way," etc.

You should now begin to see that such a test emanates once again from the re-sorting of groups of characteristics and actions and the expectation that the audience also shares this specific species of ordering.

Hugh Kenner in his book *The Counterfeiters* suggests it is no accident that the rise of narrative prose in the form of novels and stories corresponds with the cultural shift to empiricism in the late 1600s. Once we believed that what we know is derived only from the experiences our senses communicate to us, it did not take long for writers and artists of all types to begin exploring the limits of that perception. The senses, as we know from Gestalt and camouflage, can be easily fooled. So how *do* we know things?

I mentioned that Defoe published *Crusoe* as a nonfiction account. To this day it is difficult to teach "A Modest Proposal" as satire because the truth of the author's intention is so cleverly disguised by design as well as by time. Kenner explains the process of the games we play.

> Empiricism is a game. Its central rule forbids you to understand what you are talking about. The application of the rule, when we remember that we *are* playing a game, yields satire. Satire's particulars fade, its structure stays; and from within that structure a ghostly person grimaces, to catch sight of whom . . . is to command the vision which makes the whole intelligible. Bits of apparent insanity can keep us oriented: a man faking soup labels, a man writing a play about men doing nothing, a poet writing an incompetent poet's poem, a man forcing grammar and syntax to simulate . . . a few words exchanged in a New Jersey bar. These things once done seem to have unaccountably "happened" (who would take the trouble over them?), for Art too pretends to withdraw the conceiving person, while reconstituting spontaneities so that they look like behavior.

Art pretends to withdraw the conceiving person, while reconstituting the spontaneous. Sound familiar?

Here is something you can do at home. Write a bad story in the first person. In what way would that story differ from a fine, successful story narrated by an incompetent narrator? In workshop, how do we know when a thing is boring intentionally or just plain boring? It is in the confusion of form that the questions of meaning and intent play as well as questions of quality and aesthetic merit. Who hasn't squirmed while listening to readers read your stories and not wanted to rush to the defense of intention? The practice of having the author sit quietly is a way to assess the success of the author's illusion. The intention must be clear, but it must not look intentional.

"I meant the character to be dysfunctional." It is into this tangle of intention and meaning that contemporary theorists frolic, suggesting that a text's meaning, so disguised, was never really there in the first place. It is up to the reader, they say, to place an imaginary tank in a real garden. Where you have thought you placed tanks in a shroud of leaves, the reader reads the leaves. How to let the reader know that this is also a battlefield he or she gazes upon without killing him or her?

Behrens also addresses this paradox and emphasizes that in art camouflage is part of the equation. The techniques of deception are similar, but the artist's task is also to reveal that it is camouflage, that camouflage is being employed.

> The logical structure of metaphor, as Kenneth Burke implied, is A is A and not-A. It is a paradoxical or stereoscopic awareness, in which conventional organization and deviant organization are simultaneously but separately entertained in the confines of one mind. This is the structure of puns (sanity clause is and is not Santy Claus), similes (hearts are like and unlike pumps), analogies (hat is to body as attic is to house, but bodies are not houses), religious paradoxes (wine is and is not blood).

When we create Art, we invoke the not-*A* part of the equation to frame the initial comparison. We want this story we are writing to be *like* the confession of an alcoholic, but because it is read in a creative writing workshop, we proceed as if it is not. The same narrative in an AA meeting is framed differently. It is like the narrative of an alcoholic and is the narrative of the alcoholic because it takes place in this meeting. You can see, then, where the anxiety arises in workshops when the workshop as a frame becomes confused with a meeting of the AA. The frame of art can become confused for the frame of therapy because some particulars of the details of both meetings are similar — we sit in a circle, talk about feelings and our lives, etc. Or consider this example from the New York performance art world. An artist there is known for his year-long pieces. One year he intends to stay outside the entire time. Living on the streets, he equips himself with a club and is arrested by the police for carrying such a weapon. The art world intervenes to save the artist's work. The artist is like a homeless man but he is an artist, the artists say. To the police the artist is simply a homeless man.

As we create art we constantly compare two things as if they are one, feigning confusion. Camoufleurs

> use the same techniques but with a solely destructive intent. Camoufleurs only need to say that A is not-A. . . . The . . . harmlessness of creative acts is due to their double awareness in which A is A is known while A is not-A is expressed. When creative acts are framed (whether by actual picture frames, placement in museums, theatrical stages, religious edifices, scientific laboratories or tones of voice that imply a joke), they are somehow labeled as Gregory Bateson seems to say that "this is play" or "this is not a literal act." . . . Framing is essential. It separates acts of creation (which are labeled deviant acts) from such phenomena as camouflage, errors, dreaming, pornography, and madness which are unframed deviant acts.

Writing a story or hiding a tank assumes a reader with perceptual equipment that can discriminate one thing from another. Military camouflage seeks to defeat that perception, turning its limitations against its possessor, while you as an artist seek to engage that perception to entertain the possibility of discriminating a new order altogether out of the reconstructed one.

I have been talking about camouflage at the levels of language and form. Let me conclude by looking at matters of style and genre.

It is interesting that realism as a style works so diligently to conceal, as Kenner says, by withdrawing the hand of the conceiving person. Realism seeks to minimize narrative intervention of all kinds and creates, in Orwell's phrase, a kind of clear window. Paradoxically, it creates this artlessness while framed and, therefore recognizable as fiction, in the context of high art and not reality. You wouldn't catch the realist playing Defoe's satirist game of publishing out of genre or experimenting, as Robert Coover is now, with hypertext or practicing, as one contemporary sculptor does, a deception where his shard-like sculptures are buried near construction sites so that they might be discovered as evidence of a heretofore unknown civilization. Do realists seek to tell their stories in AA meetings or get them on the AP wire to be published in the nation's newspapers? Realism comes to us always presented on a field of artfulness so that its apparent artlessness is not mistaken for actual artlessness.

What are the manifestations of such a field? Hierarchies of all types. Distinctions drawn against other genres—western, science fiction, romance. The notion of genre fiction itself. The delineation between literary and popular fiction. The invention of literature itself. Publication in literary magazines and hardbacks as opposed to pulp and paperback. Publication itself. The author bio on the back flap. The MFA degree. The workshop itself. All of these settings are made clear so that the art of deception employed by realism may show forth.

This should not be surprising. As Behrens and others have stressed, we recognize things and make distinctions by means of categories. To be able to use the term *realism* or call something technically realistic is to participate in that particular act of sorting. But such sorting, as we have seen, creates blind spots in our perception. If the world is sorted into fish and reptiles, amphibians, which express characteristics of both groups, don't exist until room is made for a new grouping and the boundaries between each are redrawn.

You probably noticed that from the outset, my lecture was fraught with a certain gender anxiety, all that enthusiasm for what the military and what my own boyhood can teach us. This was partially intentional (I wrote this lecture for several reasons; nine of them are secret) in order to apply pressure to one of the border regions (gender) within which we operate.

Interestingly, gender questions surfaced early in the history of American realism. William Dean Howells, one of the innovators and propagators of the style, was also one of the first to read and distribute, in French versions, the Russian realist writers Turgenev,

Dostoevsky, and Tolstoy. Howells promoted and edited their initial English translations. My colleague John W. Crowley has pointed out that Howells immediately confronted differences between the subject matter of the Russians he admired and the particulars of the American culture he sought to enlighten. Howells was taken by the realistic treatment of war (he edited and wrote an introductory essay for Tolstoy's *Sebastopol* about the Crimean War in 1887) and the social and political struggle of the serfs and peasants because it stood in marked contrast to what was going on at home. There was a noticeable absence of interest in such subject matter in general or it was overshadowed, when expressed, with romantic set-piece writing. This situation led Howells to adapt, in his positions as editor of the *Atlantic Monthly*, tireless reviewer, and popular novelist in his own right, a domestic, in both senses of the word, realism for America. He sought to borrow, as Crowley suggests, the techniques from the Russians that express "dramatic interaction of ordinary but complex characters and with a minimum of narrative intervention—an unromanticized view of commonplace American experience." But the transplantation of such stories led him to graft those techniques to roots found in Stowe and the women's fiction of the 1850s. American experience would put its own spin on things. After all, Howells suggested, in America we don't take dissenters out to Duluth and shoot them. Unfortunately for Howells, later critics attacked him for his desire that American realism concentrate on "the smiling aspects" of life, and the boundary lines of dispute were drawn along the lines of gender. A generation later Frank Norris dismissed the realism of Howells, James, and Wharton as "the tragedy of the broken teacup."

What should you be writing about? In what manner should you write? I rehearse this little history lesson to illustrate the dynamic nature of subject matter and style, whose shifting categories are as open to argument and insight as those of point of view and tense but mainly go uncommented upon in a workshop because of the workshop's nature of perception. There may be tanks of genius sitting on our tables in our classrooms, but sometimes we cannot see them because of the apparatus of our seeing. Camouflage teaches us that we expect to see the things we see and hence we miss seeing how to see.

There is a wonderful passage in *Gravity's Rainbow* where Slothrop is wandering through the Black Forest. Suddenly he comes upon a patch of pine trees whose branches are draped with bright silver tinsel. For a moment he is confused, then he realizes at what he is looking. Bombers heading for the cities of Germany dropped strips of aluminum to confuse the echo of the enemy's radar. This bit of forest is where the camouflage had come to rest. It now camouflaged the war zone as a Christmas winter wonderland.

We are limited by the mechanism of our perceiving. Thinking about the mechanism of our perception, I hope, will help us better understand how, when we create it, fiction works. It should also remind us that the conventions of perception constantly change as well.

Let us return to the contemporary battlefield where the means of acquiring a target no longer rest in the eyes. Our technology now forces us to kill each other in a landscape sensed only at the extremes of the visual spectrum, the infrared and the ultraviolet, the whole array of electromagnetic fields and waves. Here's an image. A tank in the desert. As it moves, special mortars on the sides of the turret chuff out small bombs that explode overhead into glistening streamers of glittering chaff and sparkling dust that shower down on the vehicle. The tank cruises beneath a canopy of its own confetti. The tank looks like it is having a party. Of course, it is just a tank being stalked by radar-guided projectiles. If you were shooting at the tank, you might switch to a missile that reads the laser fingerprint you've painted on the tank's flanks. But the tank, in anticipation of such a move, has been built with a rippled surface to break up the light of the lasers, and the tank now wears a shimmering swath of rainbow. Look at that tank go! Nothing can touch it. You can't miss it. But you aren't shooting, are you? Only seeing.

The War in the Forest
THE COLLECTED WORK OF JAMES B. HALL

John Witte, the editor of *Northwest Review,* asked me to review the work of James B. Hall. This was written between the two Iraq wars, soon after Bill Clinton was elected president. I have written a few reviews—of T. C. Boyle, Stanley Elkin, John W. Crowley, Steven Milhauser, and Richard Bausch—but found I have given it up. It seems now I am writing more and more blurbs, an interesting genre of distillation.

I have been thinking about Audie Murphy. Murphy was the most decorated American soldier of World War II and died in a plane crash in 1970. I was thinking about him because Norman Schwarzkopf has been in the news again, this time submitting to interviews on television and in newspapers about his new autobiography. General Schwarzkopf always talks about parades. The parades in New York and Washington, D.C., that followed the conclusion of the Gulf War were very important to him. In talking about those parades, he always contrasts the homecoming of Vietnam War veterans who were not so honored, implying, I think, that we could have avoided a lot of the unpleasantness that dogs us now about that war if we had just given them a parade. Indeed, the image of those veterans being spat upon seems as indelibly etched in our national consciousness as the other famous pictures of the war: the gunshot to the head, the naked girl running from the napalm, the helicopter on the roof. The columnist Bob Greene, by the way, has for years offered a reward to anyone who can document a spitting incident and has so far turned up nothing. Still, the belief persists in the efficacy of some pomp (a parade and some medals) as the method of transforming soldiers back to civilians. President George H. W. Bush himself tried to extend the magic back across time as he addressed the nation and the returning Gulf War troops. "The Vietnam War," he said amazingly, "is over."

Audie Murphy was on the cover of *Life* magazine. He was nineteen years old and had won twenty-four medals including the Medal of Honor, two Silver Stars, a Bronze Star, the Legion of Merit, and the Distinguished Service Cross. He was wounded four times. The destruction of his hip kept him from going to West Point or remaining in the service. He became an actor, starring in forty or so movies. He played himself in his own story, *To Hell and Back*, where he relived, on film, the day in France when he killed single-handedly 240 Germans. Thomas B. Morgan, in his article on Murphy for the fiftieth anniversary issue of *Esquire* in 1983, recounts Murphy's heroic accomplishments but places them in the context of the wars that followed. Murphy fought in the right war. But Morgan also portrays Murphy, this most feted and welcomed-home GI, wandering the streets of Los Angeles in 1967, displaying all the symptoms of what we now think of as post-traumatic stress syndrome. Recently recovered from addiction to tranquilizers, unable to sleep for the nightmares, constantly packing an automatic, Murphy tells Morgan that it has been a long fight to keep from being bored to death. "That's what combat did to me." In the interview that follows, Murphy recounts what it feels like to have done what he has done. How many times has he told the story? And how uneasy it is, still, in the telling. The interview ends with Murphy admitting, "To become an executioner, somebody cold and analytical, to be a trained killer and then come back into civilian life and be alone in the crowd—it takes an awful long time to get over it. . . . It's been twenty odd years already. Did you know that doctors say the effect of all this on my generation won't reach its peak until 1970? So, I guess I got three years to go."

Morgan's point is that what we think of as a hero's welcome seems to be no guarantee of transition, no sure means of ameliorating what Hemingway's wounded soldier in "In Another Country" characterized as being "slightly detached." Murphy suggests that the problem stems from the home front's inability to imagine what it is they have asked their soldiers to do. This separation between those who fight and those who wait for them back home and the inability of each group to express to each other what the war has meant is an old story. Vietnam was not an anomaly. Nor will the veterans of our most recent war escape this alienation. John Keegan and Paul Fussell in their books *The Face of Battle* and *Wartime* have expertly exposed the mechanism and the ramifications of such a split on individual humans and their culture. They demonstrate that the size and lethality of twentieth century battlefields have made the drama of coming home as tragic as the war itself.

I keep thinking of Audie Murphy having to play himself in that movie. Calling down artillery on his own position, his hip going gangrenous from a wound he has suffered and refused to treat two days before, standing on the burning deck of a tank destroyer and firing at a mass of attacking German infantry. Then the director calls cut and tells him and all the dusty extras that they will have to up and do it again.

In James B. Hall's two most recent books, *Bereavements: Selected and Collected Poetry* published by Story Line Press and *I Like It Better Now: Stories* published by the University of Arkansas Press, war and its aftermath do not appear, at first, to dominate. The first thing I noticed was the range of form as well as theme. Brought out within a few months of each other, Hall's books already span two genres, but even within the prose and poetry these books further subdivide and define. Though the books are organized into various headed sections, the impression they create is that each work, poem or story, is completely unique, as if Hall had led a separate life to produce each of them. The work seeks out every niche.

There are tales and sci-fi, neo-Chekhovian and neo-Jamesian monologues, narrators who don't speak English and those who are inventing it. The poetry scans just as much territory with an array of forms both formal and improvised, dramatic, lyric, narrative, a catalog without the aftertaste of dabble nor the stale discipline of daily production. The poems are occasional in the best sense of the word, crafted without program or theory save that of an organic match. Both collections appear to be, well, collections of a remarkably voiced and multi-limbed writer who might suffer only from an excess of his own talent. But this work does not boast. The variety reflects the author's gifts.

There are individual works, however, that do confront Hall's experience in the Second World War. The story "The War in the Forest," published for the first time in *I Like It Better Now*, is a monologue delivered by an American warrant officer about the stalking of each other by Allied and German soldiers bogged down in winter woods. It is a drugged and dreamy story, incredibly brutal and precise in detail. The story pivots on the pivot of battle, the moment a combatant is captured and becomes a prisoner. This moment, like the moment of grace doled out in a Flannery O'Connor story, is an act of clarity that defines for the young soldier his true nature. In this foggy winter woods, prisoners are killed out of hand, and this is a story about the captured officer the young soldier shoots in the head. What is most moving is the loneliness of this world that is camouflaged poorly by the residue of military organization and rank. But there is no disguising the remnants of these acts. This is the squalor part of J. D. Salinger's "For Esme — With Love and Squalor," and this story takes its place beside that one as the best attempt to render that "Good War" to its elemental truths so that the rest of us can begin to understand it. In the poem "Memorial Day: 1959," Hall covers the same ground, turning the standard occasional verse on its head:

> I thought to write some formal thing
> To say how those alive — being so — see on ahead

And thought that way to justify their deaths.
But, oh, when I saw them once more, again,
I thought: write no lies to those who really died.

This poem and others, "On Pay Day Night" and "Wine of Algeria," are early approaches to the subject matter so vividly and poetically distilled in "The War in the Forest." It is in this selection of work that Hall's command of technique and genre is most easily tracked. You can see the subject matter hunting for its form, its relentless search for fit that ends where the story ends:

> After all those things, for a long time, I believed our war in the forest began and in all ways at last ended. But in fact, my war in the forest went on as it was at the onset, deeply I wished to belong but cannot belong even though I have tried to belong all the days of my life.

The "working out" that Murphy alludes to is at play. Here we understand what those doctors got wrong. The effects of the war would not really reach a peak in his generation in 1970 after all. These things aren't worked out. The year marks only the beginning of the great dying off of that generation of survivors. As I type this, the presidential campaigns are sputtering along. If, when you read this, Clinton and Gore have been elected, it will mark a true passing of the generational torch first imagined by that World War II veteran president thirty years ago. The effects of World War II on our lives were so massive and pervasive they have become almost invisible. The damage that Vietnam did to us is perhaps more obvious. The destructive reach of the World War folds into itself Vietnam and Korea, fitting them into the larger theater of that primal war, the war that never ended.

Most of Hall's poetry and prose collected here must be read in light of this. Though he seldom uses the war as direct subject matter, it is always there. In the story "But Who Gets the Children," surviving the war is close to the surface as a veteran navigates the front at home. This story is the complement to "The War in the Forest." The language of its narrator is brilliant in its fidelity to the melded jargon of corporate and military worlds. But most of the stories can be read as versions of such returns. Even the science fiction tales and fables take, as their starting points, the moments after the hollow "they lived happily ever after" part. In "A Rumor of Metal" a soldier of a postapocalyptic landscape stalks his world for any remaining metal. In the story's stunned narrative, Hall convincingly allegorizes the detachment of survival and extends veteran status to us all and on into our future. Most of the stories are positioned in this way, taking advantage of the aftermath of extreme violence. After the divorce, after the crash, after the death. There is even the imaginative extension after the end of another piece of literature. Hall has Friday tell his version of the story he finds himself in with similar poignancy and insight as Elizabeth Bishop creates in her extension of Crusoe's tale. In much the same way too, Hall uses such literary characters and dramatic monologues to mask the personal themes of alienation, losing, and returning. Hall's understanding of the intimacy of the short story form allows him to deploy his senses to best capture the precipitate of cataclysm instead of reporting only that cataclysm. We read of the explosions in the fallout. The title itself, *I Like It Better Now*, contains within it the loose formula that might define all of these stories. The stories insist upon the narrative's now and evoke the comparative. The "then" is always present within the present of the story.

Much of the poetry, too, is disguised elegy. Here again, like Bishop, form is arrayed against the pith of chaos, its control betraying itself as the last line of defense. The personas of the poems are often gleaned from other works of art. The book's program perhaps is set by the first selection in the voice of a young "Vandal," the contemporary sort, breaking into a Methodist church. This juxtaposition of sacred and profane seems on the mind of various voices, saints and characters from books including Moby Dick's mate and Jack and Jill, old poets, and emblematic types. Hall, it seems to me, stalks the ruins of civilization he has seen in ruin. He hunts. He quarries. The refrain of the title poem is "Silently, I show myself." The "I" is his ultimate costume. It is at the moments of contemplating others that he is most exposed:

But most often at home
When our five children
Talk or are all reading
Together, Oh, I miss them
So, for one moment,
Silently, I show myself.

Hall knows loss before it is gone. In a poem so domestic — about children, school, a poker game — Hall couches loss still in terms of concealment and exposure, a soldier's consciousness, displaying reluctantly the vulnerability to danger that is everywhere but also revealing himself to the self he has created.

I find fragments of what happened in those winter woods, when Hall was young and his generation was young, in everything he has written. The drama in the work springs from our collective denial that any of us could do what Hall suggests had to be done, what was done, in the war. Reading this work, we imagine a poet, a loving father, a teacher, a scholar sitting by the fire, and we also see this same character, as a young boy, place a pistol beneath the chin of a prisoner and pull the trigger. This seems an endless surprise to Hall as well and the source of his power. He survived, and he remembers. He keeps looking at that person by the fire. He keeps looking at that boy in the snowy forest. James B. Hall, in his poems and stories, continues telling the stories of an incredible truth to an audience who cannot begin to believe.

$\mathscr{A}$dventures on the Cultural Landscape
AN EPISTOLARY INTERVIEW

I have done many interviews — by telephone, e-mail, and in person. In this one, conducted by Fred Arroyo, we used the regular mail. Fred had been my student at Warren Wilson, and conducting such business by mail was an extension of the teaching that goes on in a low-residency program where packets of work are exchanged six or seven times between the instructor and the student. The interview was first published in Purdue University's *Sycamore Review* and later republished in an anthology of interviews called *Delicious Imaginations* edited by Sarah Griffiths and Kevin J. Kehrwald. Curiously, I was asked to provide a recipe to be published with the interview, though in the end it wasn't published in the book. I contributed a recipe for making marshmallows.

This interview is the product of two separate written documents. Fred Santiago Arroyo mailed Michael Martone a series of questions, some of which focus on his own aesthetic obsessions and some which he thought were "appropriate for an interview." Michael Martone then wrote out his responses to Fred's questions and sent them to *Sycamore Review*. There was only one exchange between Fred and Michael; this epistolary interview seeks to preserve the friction and energy between what Fred asked and what Michael chose to answer — or ignore.

Question 1.   Readers will see two general notions concerning your fiction and your life. First, you steadily write new stories, but in your most recent collections—*Fort Wayne Is Seventh on Hitler's List* and *Seeing Eye*—you combine new stories with work previously published in your first two collections. Second, you spend a lot of time teaching fiction writing. Could you talk about the relationship between writing and teaching? Does teaching adversely affect your writing, or does teaching help your fiction?

It seems, in the two parts of your question, that what you are really getting at has to do with a correlation between the amount of time and effort one spends on one's work and the corresponding expenditure of time and effort on one's job. Also that the amount of "new" writing is somehow connected to the writing that is somehow "good."

I have been writing and publishing for twenty years and have produced a limited (it is always limited in some way) amount of work; republishing some of it from book to book implies that the creation of new work is more time-consuming than the republishing or the maintaining in print work previously published. I am not sure that is the case. The creation of places to publish is as time-consuming to me and just as creative. The way I view publishing is that it is up to me to keep as much of all my work in print as long as possible. Who else will? At the same time I am creating new work, I am maintaining the old. Maintaining is a difficult thing to do. After the Troy Tool decision rendered by the Supreme Court, commercial presses were forced to refocus their business. The backlist, which had been their asset, was now a liability. My first book published by Knopf was in print only nine months before it was remaindered. Given this kind of environment, it seems to me the author must take on more of the responsibility of publishing his or her own work and maintaining its availability. I have had more success in that way of course with university and nonprofit presses and in publishing my own work.

More theoretically, I do think of all this work, all these individual stories, as part of one big work that is constantly evolving and mutating. Also many of the individual pieces are themselves constructed in a collage style, by arrangement of components. So juxtaposition on that micro level is important to me as it is on a macro level. The Dan Quayle pieces read differently in their chapbook from when they are the middle third of *Seeing Eye*. Both readings interest me and I hope will interest readers. I like to think I do not just create objects that are separate from their contexts. I also create or help create their contexts.

To make the transition to teaching, I believe that this is one thing not taught so much in workshops or in writing programs. That is, we treat the story or poem under consideration in class as this detached piece, the object on the table, and ignore the contexts of where and why it will be published or how it will be read or used or how the changing frame of how it is read changes the way it is read. How framing contributes to the meaning of the piece is rarely discussed in workshops. That is why I have a large component of "framing" discussion in my class. My students must self-publish some of their own work for example. We don't discuss how to get published so much as what publishing means, its history, its material effect and contribution to what we think of as literature. The idea and invention of "Literature" itself. I try to go beyond a class that is simply about judgment: This poem is better than this poem. This story works. This piece needs polishing.

The writer, for me, is not simply the producer of raw material, uncut stone, say, or, a little beyond that, a mere producer of gem-like stone, but is also the contributor and manipulator of the setting of the jewel. We do read a book by its cover. But traditionally programs have shied away from discussions of this sort. We talk about the creation of the art but not the self-creation of the artist. The creation of a self as an artist and hence the artist's role in culture is as interesting to me as the individual artifact of poem or story. Isn't that, the creation of the artist, what the form of the author interview is all about? The interview as a piece of creative writing not just about creative writing.

So you can see that teaching affects my work, the work affects my teaching.

What surprises me is that you didn't ask about my family. I have had small children around me for a while. My time and my ideas about time, what is important or not, what is good or bad for me and for the world have certainly shifted because of that. Having small children has affected my work, but I tend not to mark it as adverse or helpful.

I tend not to think in those terms because I do not know what is ultimately good or bad when it comes to my work. It is something I live with, something that you live with too with your work. I think trying to judge yourself at the same time you are trying to do something can drive you crazy. I may have written my "best" work already, but I am looking at twenty more years of work. I don't know. My "best" work may be written two years from now, but what if I die next month in a car wreck before I get to that "best" piece of writing? These thoughts would be truly debilitating if the reason I wrote was to write "good" stuff or if my only purpose was to get "better."

Now a car wreck might adversely impact my work, right, but then again, my death might actually be helpful to my work because my readers, such as yourself, would reset my work in the context of my death. Don't know. What I am saying is that I don't fret about this question beyond the point of how one thing changes another. I like the physics of the break more than the occasional drop of the balls in the pocket. When it does happen it is both accident and skill. I tend, then, not to judge those changes as good or bad. You can't know ultimately.

Question 2.   I asked my last question because there is a continual concern regarding the function of creative writing programs — questions about whether they are doing more harm than good, and what will happen to all these people with MFAs. Being a graduate from the Writing Seminars at Johns Hopkins and having taught so long, how do you approach these concerns?

Who is continuously concerned with this? Who sits up nights and worries about programs doing harm? To what? Great literature? Moral fiber? Financial return? Who is it who worries? That's a question. No doubt of the fact of the massive growth of MFA programs, writing classes, etc. But their harm or good? C'mon.

The real problem for me is that writing programs don't study themselves as a cultural manifestation and describe the changes that they have wrought in the production of literature, reading practices, publishing apparati, connection to other forms of narrative delivery devices, etc. Programs are so detached from the real question of the consequences of their existence. Creative Writing has been around in this form for fifty years, and all this question worries about is: is it good or bad? Which merely replicates what seems to be the big question in most individual workshops. Is this story or poem good or bad? To me that is the least interesting question.

Isn't the assumption in your question somehow related to the notion of standards? That those people who decide to write are also charged as some kind of priests of the good and the beautiful. I would like to think that writers and artists before they were in the academy didn't worry so much about the decline of standards. It is the academy itself, an institution that is founded on making distinctions, passing judgment, creating hierarchies that has made writers overly conscious of their function as defenders of what is good instead of simply makers of art. That is, your very question emanates from the culture of the academy. Are standards falling? Writers in the university must be very careful. They must negotiate the role imposed on them to be gatekeepers, assayers, and critics. Writers who teach should not come to feel they actually know what is great art or great writing and will transfer the knowledge to the humble student. But that is the way universities function. Universities by nature get bogged down in the question of maintaining standards in degraded times. It's Dark Ages stuff; it's where the institution evolved. In universities we always live in the age of lead.

The real question for me is what is this thing, this artifact? And, after that, given what thing this thing is, what is it doing in a larger context? Your question — are programs doing more harm than good — suggests you already know what writing has done in the world, what it does in the world now, and what it should continue to do. I am not so sure.

I find it amazing that programs have never really discovered what their students do get from the programs and the classes they attended. Very little follow-up surveying, say, though there is an interesting one going on now at Syracuse being done by Vincent Standley. What makes a program successful? Gee, I guess, if we think about it at all, I guess programs think they are successful if their graduates publish and go on to teaching as well. But I have a feeling, and it is a feeling because there is no data, natch (where is the AWP when they really are needed?), that people have used their time in the program, their program degrees, for a variety of unimaginable diverse things. It is a recurring theme for me here that the administration of imaginative writing is always a failure of imagination of what it is up to. Imaginative writing programs cannot imagine the ways people read for a variety of reasons beyond just whether something is good or bad.

You know why leather-bound books from the nineteenth century often come to us now with water circles on their covers? Because the books were used as plant stands by their owners. Books as status objects. This kind of study, which considers the book and writing as cultural artifact as well as aesthetic object, interests me more than the righteous culling of the good from the bad.

We want to rush to judgment before we even know what the phenomenon is. Buried in this question of good or bad is the assumption that the writer or artist is simply the producer of the cultural object. But that isn't true. We are both the producers and consumers of cultural objects, and within the objects we produce we create characters like ourselves who produce and consume culture. And this activity in the world goes on without the constant assessment of its goodness or badness being the primary or ultimate activity. I don't believe in progress so much as I believe in change. It has never been my job (even when I went into teaching) to be a caretaker, a gatekeeper, a fiduciary trustee of knowledge, a role model.

Maybe, just maybe, creative writing programs really aren't about producing good or bad writing in the way the book in the nineteenth century was not for reading but for plant standing and status display. Or maybe I am teaching my students how to make good plant stands. And, by gum, I am going to be the best teacher of plant stand making I can be, and they will make the best plant stands imaginable.

Maybe it is not about producing literature at all, good or bad, but about producing, say, lawyers. English departments, by the way, produce more lawyers than literary scholars, for good or bad, depending on your POV. So the question might be are English departments the best way to produce bad lawyers or the worst way to produce good ones?

Whatever writing programs are, they can seem to be successful or awful for a given context. That can change. And it is that—what they do and how they change—that should be some of the object of our study beyond the simple question of good or bad copy. I think it's good that people, all kinds of people, write, write all kinds of stuff, or that these people are finding ways to struggle with the problems of writing. I think it is good that many people find intrinsic value and enjoyment in the process of writing. I encourage that. I think a space should be made to allow for this activity. I just don't take the next step. That people who write and find pleasure in that should also only write in one way, a "good" way, and that that good be the only measure and worth of the activity.

Question 3.   I see a relationship between this first set of questions and the way you approach fiction—the way you use first person; personas, monologues, and voices; history and historical figures; and the geography of Indiana—which always decisively draws me to see that you are telling a story. Often, it's as if you're stressing the need to *tell* a story rather than the urgency of telling a *story*. I know it is hard to separate your form from your content, and yet I feel you are telling a story, showing me how to read it, and, since I am a writer, how to consider writing

fiction. In other words, it's as if you're teaching me. Do you see this or consider this in your fiction?

You're right. This question is related. As you might guess, I am not just interested in writing a story that somehow stands alone. I am interested in the context of the story, the frame in which it is read. I don't really write stories. I think of what I do as creating fictions. Fictional characters based on actual people, for example, who then really "write" or "tell" in a kind of essay-like ramble. Often the thing these fictional or fictionalized characters want to talk about is getting trapped within, between fiction and real worlds.

Currently I am working on some series of fictions that attempt to "pass" as nonfiction. I am writing a travel guide to Indiana and have been publishing sections in newspapers and magazines without framing them as fiction.

I am also writing poems under the name of "Neal Bowers." Another Neal Bowers, who you might know, has written a book published by Norton about his search for someone who plagiarized his poems. I am not using Bowers's poems, only the name "Neal Bowers" as my pen name. So when these poems get published, Neal Bowers could actually include them on his vita as far as I am concerned. I hope he does. This fiction asks the certain questions I hate to see go begging. What is authorship? What is the authentic? What does it mean to be original? What is real and what is counterfeit? In the particular case, I understand the theft of intellectual property that got Neal Bowers so worked up. But is it plagiarism to actually contribute to someone else's work? I am not stealing his work but actually donating my own to his store of work.

I think all stories finally are about the act of storytelling, are about fiction. Even the most realistic realists working so hard to make their fictions appear as if they are real and not artifice, scoffing at formalists and experimental writers for their tricks and their self-consciousness, encode their own work with stories about stories, fiction about fiction. I think the binary between realists and postmodernists (or whatever) is inexact. Realism as a fictional style is exhausted not by the critique of other more openly self-conscious fiction but by the forms of memoir and autobiography. Realism is the biggest fake of all. It tries so hard to look like a poorly written memoir or a celebrity biography while all the time it is winking furiously to let us know it is fiction and not simply a poorly written memoir.

Right, all narratives come with their own sets of instructions on how to read them, not just mine. And readers are amazing. I love to watch them calibrate their reading to what it is they are reading. Sometimes it works, sometimes not. But readers are savvy sorters—sniffing out fakes from fakes, good parodies from bad non-parodies. There is that good and bad again. My favorite annual department meeting is when an entire faculty grades the same freshman comp paper. The responses are everywhere on the bell curve.

Question 4. You once said something that I continually return to and which has become, in my own paraphrase, very crucial to writing: Perhaps we create characters who write essays. Our fiction is in the creation of a character—the character writes philosophy. Sometimes people just read fiction, then, as philosophy or essay; perhaps what is created should not be called novels or stories but extended prose narratives or simply fictions (*ficciones*). Could you explain further? Which writers drew you to this notion of fiction and how it relates to the historical and literary epoch we live in and are traveling toward?

Perhaps more than any fiction writer, Hugh Kenner got me thinking in terms of fictions. There is a wonderful writer and artist named Roy Behrens whose work on camouflage and art is important to me. He publishes an amazing 'zine called *Ballast* on visual and verbal punning. The photographs of Cindy Sherman. Chuck Jones cartoons, especially *Duck Amuck* and the Brothers Quay animation. The novels of Marx and Freud. The songs and singing of Yma Sumac. The industrial design of Raymond Loewy and the photographs of O. Winston Link. *The Big Book* of AA. A film called *La Jetée*. The work of J. G. Ballard. *Duplex Planet*. The comic books of Harvey Pekar. Joseph Cornell. The architecture of Rogers and Piano, Gehry, and Graves. The ruined city of Detroit and the imaginary ones of Indianapolis and Gary. Thucydides. Alice and Edith Hamilton. Thomas Kuhn. Philo T. Farnsworth and Chester Carlson. Beckett, Borges, Barth, Barthelme, Calvino, Davenport, Gass, Hardy, Stein, Elkin, the whole modernist trading card collection. Richard Rhodes and John McPhee. Cole Porter, WOWO radio, Captain Kangaroo and Mr. Rogers. The novels of Alfred Kinsey. Harry Gonzo. John Cougar and Tom Waits. O. Henry, Saki, Jackson, and whoever wrote "The Lady, or the Tiger" along with the whole seventh grade unit on the short story, which has not changed from the beginning of time.

I saw John Barth do something very interesting when he came to this question, the one I am answering now. There is always the question about influences. You asked specifically about writers, but Barth, who often writes his own interview questions and I think never does actual "live" interviews, had the influence question couched as "What are you reading?" So instead of answering the implied question "Whom influential are you reading?" he took it literally. He started by saying he read the newspaper; he listed magazines and catalogs he subscribed to, mail he read, cereal boxes. He then listed road signs and billboards, department memos, student composition papers, student fiction papers, graduate student fiction, former graduate students who had sent to him their work now published, galleys sent by publishers looking for a blurb, advance copies, desk copies, review copies, reviews themselves, the literary journals that are sent to him or he subscribes to. Then he said he reads what he himself has written the day before when he sits down to write that day. And he reads his own already published books occasionally as well as books he purchased in bookstores, etc. A clever answer of course, but I realized that it is a far more accurate picture of a literate life, a reading life, and it is about influences as well.

I love how this clever answer asks the question. What is the interviewer really asking? Again it seems to me that the assumptions about influences often suggest the notion of a Gatsby-like program of improvement. The writer only reads "good" books that contribute to his or her scheme of perfection. Or, even better, the writer simply displays the "good" books in public view but never actually reads them.

Whatever I am up to as a writer has come about mainly by accident, inertia, and least resistance. I can't imagine that the important books I have read, movies I've seen, etc., would be of any value to anyone else *necessarily*. The reading I have done that has been influential has come to me because I have happened upon it (okay, okay, I read about some of it in author interviews), run into it. It has been on hand or at hand. Reading is important to me, so I read as much as I can. Perhaps the question is meant to be a short circuit in order to avoid all the stuff I have read that had absolutely no influence, only the good stuff. But, as Barth implies, everything you read is processed in some way. Ya never know.

This question got me thinking about form again. The form of the interview, the interview as fictional form. My reading tells me P. T. Barnum invented the interview or profile as we know it, and it was used as self-promotion, of course. It was used fictionally first, I believe, by W. D. Howells, a writer I like to read when I have the chance.

Question 5. In the essay "Schizopsychology," under the subheading "Material for the Formation of a Plot," the Yugoslavian writer Danilo Kiš writes the following:

Stories like the one about Boris Davidovich or any other from *A Tomb for Boris Davidovich* must submit more or less all their data to what Marguerite Youcenar would call "the touchstone of fact." In other words, the author must renounce arbitrary fabrication (for, literary conventions notwithstanding, he is treating a historical topic and historical characters, sometimes under their own names, sometimes as a kind of identikit picture) *in favor of documents and historical facts*; above all, on the level of what Shklovsky calls fibula or "story." ("Story is in fact merely material for the formation of plot," says Shklovsky.) I was forced, (then) when choosing topics for my cycle, to make use of raw material, "stories" in the Shklovskian sense, whose authenticity could not be doubted. (*Homo Poeticus* 54–55) [emphasis Arroyo's]

Does this relate at all to the way you approach your fiction? So many of the stories in *Fort Wayne Is Seventh on Hitler's List*—if not the whole collection and its title—relate to what Kis is discussing.

I don't know Kiš, but now I've got to read him.

I love the idea of residue, the notion that fiction is a thing made while fact is a thing done. In that way fiction, the thing made, is "realer," while facts, once they are done, leave only traces of physical residue, and that residue can be manipulated, faked. Kenner points out that once our culture makes a shift toward the empirical, that is, what we know we know only by sense perception, it follows very quickly that the senses we are counting on to know can be fooled quite easily. What follows is satire and an explosion of fabrications, counterfeits, fakes, and hoaxes. And once those satires are in the world, the particulars of what is being satired fade away, and what is left is the scaffolding of the joke. The Irish famine is a fact done, but "A Modest Proposal" still exists. So it is very hard to tell art from its parody, satirical excess from impassioned plea.

I like this notion of document. The most telling utterance of the century is, perhaps, "Your papers, please." I like the art where there are no pictures other than just the pictures of stamps and seals and signatures authenticating the picture.

Or look at a recent edition of "The Yellow Wallpaper," which comes encased within all these essays and framing narratives.

Reading is a sifting through documents, idioms, fragments, and through layers of time and lingering memories of previous readings. I like to think of the writer more as an arranger or curator than as an originating genius.

Most of my story "Schliemann in Indianapolis" I did not "write." The text was found in a journal the archaeologist kept while in Indianapolis in the 1870s. Eli Lilly, the inventor of the gelatin capsule, edited the edition I found. Schliemann himself reconstructed Knossos from the fragments he found, letting his imagination act as a mortar between the parts. In my story about him I wrote only some of the sections between his writing, trying to blend those sections together with a seamlessness into a more complete "actual" document, which was itself about archaeology, history, divorce and marriage.

The story then is for me a kind of museum, sometimes with labels, other times just unlabeled in a pack of other documents. And a published book of stories is also about the blurbs and the flap copy, the fiction that accompanies the fiction inside. Remember P. T. Barnum was the inventor of the museum as well as the interview.

What I am making finally is a real artifact as well as the abstraction called a story. Though not as obvious as if I were making a painting or sculpture, there is a material reality to what I make.

I love the fact that my students now rigged up with an incredible, powerful typesetting tool, the computer, employ all that technology to make their typescript look like it was banged out on an old manual typewriter. Isn't it amazing that if someone gets clever in the creation of a story document, switching fonts and stuff, breaking conventions and arranging the prose in two or more columns, using punctuation, for God's sake, most workshops will usually shout it down? Manipulation of the physical object is thought to be merely clever at best. The expected workshop response is to ignore the package, to encourage the clear-window written style, to pretend the physical package is absent completely. That's not where the action is, that is not where "creative" writing resides. Writers usually abdicate the packaging to others. And writers don't work well with others in the collaboration of the making of the thing. Creative writing programs actually encourage not working well with others, I think, by making writing a competitive sport—who is the best writer of his or her generation, that kind of stuff. Sure writers would like it to look "nice," but often that is as far as the thinking goes. The job of the writer, they think, is to think up the best words in the best order. The material manipulation is left to others who are subordinates, I think they think.

Question 6. **I see Indiana, in Kiš's terms, as a "document," a "touchstone of fact." So what about Dan Quayle—does he become a document? Because you use his persona, does the reader ultimately enter your fiction with a set of assumptions? And does your fiction verify those assumptions, the "touchstone of fact" surrounding Dan Quayle? It seems to me that once I enter into the document I lose sight of the real Dan Quayle; I enter a new world where your monologues transform or transcend my old assumptions. Do you believe that history and historical figures can be reimagined to create new meaning?**

I guess I think that both Indiana and Dan Quayle don't exist. They don't exist, in a way, until the story is written about them. We talk about a sense of place or a sense of history as if we mean some people have a special gift to perceive something "out there." I feel it is more about *making* "place" or making "history." It isn't about passive reception but active creation. What Indiana is for some people is what I and other writers have made of it. Ditto Dan Quayle. Dan Quayle has not just been written by me. And my writing of Dan Quayle both creates him and reacts with other writing done to create Dan Quayle.

My chapbook of Quayle stories was published on the same day as his memoir. The *Indianapolis Star,* his family newspaper, never reviewed my book as a fiction or a collection of stories but covered its publication as a sidebar news story to the publication event of a real memoir. My book, a little fake memoir, was seen as a news story not literature. It attached itself to all these other texts about his book, little pilot fish on the belly of the shark.

That's the thing, isn't it? How do you "know" Dan Quayle or Indiana, for that matter? Most of us know through the reading, the processing of information. And even if we haul our sensing equipment to an actual place, say a dinner with the veep, there is still a lot of interpretation you must engage in. You read. I liked to think about my Dan Quayle watching television where comics are telling jokes about Dan Quayle. Historical real figures are reimagined all the time by others and by themselves, I imagine.

You know the old saw about writing what you know? But there has been a long-running fight about what experience is the important experience to render. South Seas adventure or "the tragedy of the broken teacup." You have writers who work so hard to actually collect experience or critics who lament the fact that writers don't ditch-dig anymore. Writer and writing as anthropologist. Bring the strange real thing back alive. Now, a report from Paducah, Kentucky! That's all well and good. But it still goes into words. There has always been this virtual reality of reading. Reading as an important primary experience.

Question 7. Indiana plays such a key role as a document in your writing. Yet you lived in Iowa quite a while, and then Syracuse, New York, before recently moving to Alabama. First, how did you return imaginatively to the Midwest when you lived away from it for a long period of time? Second, now that you have moved to Alabama, are there any new documents you see? Are you beginning to see your relationships and ties to the Midwest changing?

Part of returning imaginatively for me means I had relatively few other stories about Indiana to fight through or absorb or transform. Now that I am in the South, what strikes me is how writers wishing to write about it struggle with not only the stories written of the region but the actual enactment of the stories real southerners have read and now perform.

Flannery O'Connor recalls the time where she corrects a teacher about his misreading of the grandmother in "A Good Man Is Hard to Find." The teacher has transformed the grandmother into a symbol; she stands for a witch, evil. She even has a cat. O'Connor instructs the instructor that his students' reluctance to concur

with the reading might have something to do with the actual realistic portrayal of the grandmother. The students all have aunts
or grandmothers like this woman their teacher sees as a witch so
hesitate to extend that insight to their own lives. That is to say,
it is hard to say here in the South whether the story, any story, is
a mere reflection of the region and its people or if the story has
actually by its reading served as a kind of manual for behavior for
Southerners. Chicken or egg kind of thing. The feedback loop
running in the South between its composers of stories and its readers of stories is quite complex.

Philip Roth reflected on this in his essay on writing American
fiction suggesting how difficult it is because reality and the other
narrative media — newspapers, television, radio, etc. — are so in-
ventive. He suggests that a fiction writer is, well, envious, say, of
the creation of the character Richard Nixon.

The job of "writer" in the Midwest and especially "midwestern
writer" does not seem nearly as visible as that of the southerner.
That goes for "midwestern reader of midwestern writer" as well.
Not the critical mass. People seem curious about writing about the
Midwest. Most people of course would never think about asking
why anyone would write about the South. It is a bonafide story
land. That's a place where stories happen. Stories don't seem to
happen in the Midwest, most would believe. But as I said above,
stories happen when writers write them. This chicken does come
before the egg for me.

So it's easy for me to write about the Midwest. A relative clear
canvas unencumbered by narratives either inscribed or acted out.
I get to make things up or tell the truth, and readers both in the
region and beyond will be surprised since Indiana is invisible in
a way. The joke of the travel guide to Indiana is not only that no
one else in the country tours Indiana in the same way they tour
Milan or Paris or New York or New Orleans, but that Hoosiers
themselves don't know Indiana. Most natives of Fort Wayne, I
imagine, have a better cognitive map of Manhattan or L.A. thanks
to the narratives they've read or seen than they do of Indianapolis,

where they might have visited. I get to make the maps that never existed.

My Indiana finally is only my Indiana. I like to think that stories infect their readers. A kind of virus. I'd like to think that if an Indiana reader actually does pick up one of my stories, my coded message of Indiana will begin to rearrange the perception of the place by the one in place and then go on to actually change the place itself through the informed actions of the one infected by the stories.

Question 8.   Is a writer's place his destiny?

Perhaps. Place has certainly been important to me as a subject matter, as a lens. But there are other filters through which one can sift one's destiny as a writer surely. I am an Italian-American and have sometimes received solicitations to contribute to a magazine in your neck of the woods, *VIA*, which publishes work by Italian-American writers. But that way of thinking of myself, my ethnicity, has not been as important as my nativity.

The story in my family is that my Italian grandfather on the train from New York to Chicago got off in Fort Wayne thinking it was Chicago and stayed. I like that story.

When I taught at Syracuse University, the faculty in the English department was deeply engaged in this question, arguing for and against various champions as the one defining destiny. They liked to call this defining characteristic the "site of contestation." Possible candidates: race, class, gender, ethnicity, and sexual preference. As I said, the university is all about finding and defending absolutes. It is curious that place or region did not, at Syracuse, make it on the hit parade of possible destiny determinants. Curious because the local, place, is still linked, in our democracy, to the actual legal determination of power. The vote is granted to you by where you are. The political power of place then seems more real in some ways than that of race, gender, etc.

Isn't your question about who we are or who a writer is *first*? And it also is about how any one of us sees others and what we

see first when we look at others — skin color, sexual characteristics, occupation and income, etc. So again the notion of "passing" comes up in my mind. How much of my Indiana-ness is only
passing since, as you have mentioned, I have lived out of state as
much as I have lived in it. I am just thinking once again about
the artifice part of all these distinctions, their meanings affixed
culturally instead of absolutely. That is not to say that the consequences of being perceived through constructed categories aren't
real. I guess I am saying these constructed categories do become
very real. Maybe place is not every writer's destiny, but every writer
must understand place in the geographical sense and the notion of
place-ness in all the social and political senses. Yes, a writer must
know his or her place.

Question 9.   *In A Place of Sense: Essays in Search of the Midwest*
you write about "The Flatness." Some get out of the Midwest
and can't "see what is all around them now. A kind of blind-
ness afflicts them, a pathology of the path. The flatness" (29).
I remember you once told me the importance of flatness: if we
continue to sand and rub down a plane of wood, it does get flat-
ter, but it also begins to gain depth, we begin to see and feel. I
see this in your essay when you tell us:

> I dislike the metaphor of the Heartland . . . I think of it more as a web
> of tissue, a membrane, a skin. And the way I feel about the Midwest
> is the way my skin feels and the way I feel my own skin — in layers
> and broad stripes and shades, in planes and in the periphery. The
> Midwest as hide, an organ of sense and not power, delicate and
> coarse at the same time. The Midwest transmits in fields and waves.
> It is a place of sense. It sometimes differentiates heat and cold, pain
> and pleasure, but most often it registers the constant bombard-
> ment, the monotonous feel of feeling. Living here on the great flat
> plain teaches you this soft touch. Sensation arrives in huge sheets,
> stretched tight, layer upon layer, another kind of flood. . . . *I grew
> up in a landscape not often painted or photographed. The place is more
> like the materials of art itself — the stretched canvas and paper. The*

*Midwestern landscape is abstract, and our response to the geology of
the region might be similar to our response to the contemporary walls
of paint in the museums. We are forced to live in our eyes, in the outposts of our consciousness, the borders of our being. Forget the heart.
In the flatness, everywhere is surface.* (33) [emphasis Arroyo's]

Personally, Michael, I want to tell you how right and true this
feels to me. Even though my parents have moved to Puerto Rico,
and I look on the Midwest and sometimes see only all that is
gone, all that has not been "painted and photographed," I know
I was born in and will always be a part of the Midwest. Reading
your passage shows me how much is here for me and for others — how much we can still find on the surface. What are things
you tried to find to bring to the "surface," that you tried to see
and "sense"? Will there always be something to rise out of the
flatness for you?

I was trying in that passage to actually describe the physical
place and wedge off some of the adhering narrative. My teacher
Scott Sanders, I know, disagrees with my extreme notion that the
writer makes the place, that place does not exist before the writer.
He points out, rightly, I think, that we are indeed clever animals
(and it is that quality I have been thinking most about for this
interview) but that the world, nature, etc., exist beyond us as well
and will exist after we disappear.

To be a regional writer is to be faced with focusing upon both
the natural landscape and the massaged one that clever humans
have been manipulating for years. To even say there is an "Indiana"
is to say you are at least several layers away from what is really
there. Where I am certainly a cultural regionalist, fascinated by the
residue of human infestation of a part of the planet, Scott then, I
think, is a regionalist engaged with the measure of consequence
this human inhabitation has wrought upon the something other
than human. We both get lost in our paradoxes. There is something more real than the metaphor, and metaphor can become
very real.

The words you emphasize are related to what I have been trying to articulate above. That is, what interests me more is the recording and the making of sensation than the ultimate processing and storing of data. When I read and when I am not reading, just hanging out, I want my first and perhaps last response to be curiosity. Hey and isn't that a Midwestern cliché? The gawking yokel in the big city staring up at the big buildings, saying howdy on the mean streets to strangers. That's me. I am less interested in the more critical function or establishing a platform from which I can deliver verdicts. I resist being an expert. Perhaps that is why I've resisted answering some of these questions in a straightforward way. Still collecting data.

The Midwest for me has been an environment, a scape that nurtures curiosity in me. It has the possibility for a kind of openness to experience. Yes, yes, it also has its boundaries, but I make a big deal of how as an actual physical region we haven't even agreed where it is, what states belong in the Midwest. I adore the fluidity of that, how sometimes Oklahoma is midwestern, or Kentucky. Then those places aren't. At the annual conference of midwestern literature, the papers all reflect this; a portion is always given over to defining where the Midwest is for this particular presentation before the paper can get on with its subject. The Midwest is sliding around on a very active plate tectonic, a little cultural crust of earth. Curiosity, amazement, surprise, juxtaposition can still exist for me in the place called the Midwest.

Question 10.   What does it mean to be an Indiana or midwestern writer? Is there a sense of regionalism involved, and is this a negative connotation? Or is there something good about knowing one's region?

Regionalism as an ism was made negative in this century when the creation of a national literature became important politically. Virgil got busy writing the epic for Rome as Rome got interested in expanding. American literature got invented looking backward and got used by people to prove a point that America was now a nation like our competitors, or at least it seems to me. You guys have a navy, now we have a navy. You guys have great books, and see, we do too. Hey, if the standard becomes world-class, the regional is not contributing except of course as raw material to refresh the national treasure.

I have a friend who made her living strip-mining the Midwest of old clothes. She would go to small towns where family-owned department stores were going out of business and buy the whole stock, often discovering unopened treasures warehoused from the fifties and sixties, buying the stuff for pennies on the pound. She would in turn sell the stuff, reframed as nostalgic, retro clothing, in trendy shops in the border towns of New York and L.A. Context and reframing. At a dinner party in Boston, I, a newly arrived midwesterner self-conscious bumpkin trying to pass as a sophisticated urbanite, complimented the host on his delicious chocolate mousse only to be told it was chocolate pudding and that regional cooking was now haute cuisine. An old story.

Again, in your question is the hidden voice of the person or persons making the judgment, connoting the connotation. It's there of course, but these judgments certainly aren't final or for all time. That regionalism does have a negative connotation proves my point, I think. People use that art and literature for other purposes beyond reading the aesthetic delight. Powerful people and institutions use the notion of a national literature in the way homeowners displayed books as plant stands. The old standards often are standards solely and never read. A lot of people bought William Bennett's book filled, he says, with virtue, but it might just have been virtuous enough to buy the book and to have it on the shelf.

And I would be curious to know how many copies of, say, Carolyn Chute's book *The Beans of Egypt, Maine* resting on the bookshelves of the cottages of summer people were first picked up only because Maine was in the title. The reading and the use of that book, as I have suggested, seems wonderfully complex and provokes questions far beyond its goodness as a piece of writing.

Being a regionalist forces you, I would think, to consider the ramifications of political power, to consider questions of propaganda and the control and purpose of national or ethic mythmaking. Writing about region will be used to define region, who is in it and who is outside it.

Question 11.   If given the opportunity (and perhaps you've already had it), would you return to Indiana to teach and write? Do you think it would help your fiction or hinder it?

I think you would know by now that help or hinder is not in my calculations so much as staying attuned to the forces that deflect or inform what I do write. Would coming to Indiana be the best setup? Who's to say?

One of the great dramas for me in literature is the conflict between mobility and staying put. I see it everywhere. In our lives and in the stories we tell about our lives.

n Memory of Richard Cassell

This eulogy was written for a memorial service held at Butler University in 1992. It was later published in the university's literary magazine, *Manuscripts*. I was a student at Butler from 1973 to 1976. The campus is near Indianapolis's famous cemetery, Crown Hill, the final resting place of James Whitcomb Riley and John Dillinger among many others.

And then the Windows failed — and then
I could not see to see —
EMILY DICKINSON

When I was going to school at Butler in the mid-1970s, I lived in Ross Hall on the third floor in the front, above the main door, with a window that looked out onto Hampton Street and the campus beyond. My roommate, Bob Sullivan, another English major, was trying to decide whether to follow Thomas Merton into the Trappist monastery or pledge the Tekes. To help him decide, he would make retreats to the abbey in Kentucky from time to time or disappear for days after a party at the house. Consequently, I was often left alone, perched in the dorm. The dorms were closed then, locked up tight at night. If one was not organized in a Greek house or didn't have a car, the highlight of the weekend would be watching David Letterman make fun of Jane Pauley while they did the news and weather at WISH TV on the big set in the basement common room. Then, after that, along with twelve other bored guys, one would recite the lines from *Star Trek,* committed to memory, as the reruns played on TV, Captain Kirk patiently explaining to another confused alien that "Man must struggle!"

I spent a lot of time in my room, reading. The chimes from the Holcomb Tower or, more often the case, the thumping refrain from "Stairway to Heaven" booming from the speakers in the windows of the Sigma Chi house next door would draw me to my window, and I would watch the traffic putter by below while dipping into Hardy's Wessex and reading about Tess's search for legitimacy and love.

Professor Cassell did not know I watched him from that window as he paraded home until I slipped and spilled my secret when I read my fiction at Butler last year. I'd see him emerge from Jordan and plot a tangent that would take him across the parkway and the open field, where the new dorm is now, to an intersection with Hampton at the corner of Sunset. He moved as stately as a ship and, seen head-on from my vantage, his features were as sharp as a ship's prow or as thin as the seam a mold leaves in a figure of chocolate or lead. At that angle he did seem almost two-dimensional. Egyptian, with his briefcase, as heavy as a tool bag, plumb and steady at his side. His walk was a mixture of Groucho Marx and the samurai in Kurosawa films, all bounce in the knees with the legs flexed. He led with his chin, his pipe clenched in his teeth, a cross between Popeye and FDR. His face was as streamlined as a locomotive designed by Raymond Loewy, the beard scoured metallic, the forehead smoothed, the hair sculpted, Poundian and pounding for home, his head pulsing forward on his thin neck.

Suddenly he was right below me. And then black felt derbies orbited around him in the air. They settled at his feet like fat crows. Squealing sorority women and fraternity men burst about him. The women snatched at the derbies, tried to carry them away for charity. Dr. Cassell never broke stride, negotiated a course through this Sargasso of undergraduates. I watched until I could see him no more as he slouched toward home.

This last winter I flew out to Butler to do a program, and Susan

Neville, my friend and a professor there, picked me up at the airport. I was already thinking then what I would try to write here. Driving into Butler, we went by Lafayette Mall, and I remembered I had bought my first wool topcoat (blue herringbone and padded shoulders, the works) from a huge used clothing store in that neighborhood when I was a student at Butler. I bought the coat, of course, because I wanted, just a little, to look like Professor Cassell. The topcoat added to the impressive superstructure of those daily processions I witnessed. I studied with Dr. Cassell, it is true, but most of all I studied him.

Yes, it was in a night class he taught, a course on the short story, where I first read William Gass's "In the Heart of the Heart of the Country," and it changed my life and started me writing my own stories about Indiana. But I can't really remember anything specific he taught me about anything, any information or insight on texts. I turned out to be a writer, not a scholar. What Professor Cassell gave was not knowledge of characters in books but an interest in character itself and by extension a fascination with life, especially the minute gestures of living.

The film director John Ford said of John Wayne, "Dammit, he just looked like a man!" So it was with this man. He might have been a brilliant scholar, probably was. He might have been an insightful critic, probably was. I don't know. I don't remember. I remember his bearing, his manner, his physical presence in the classroom, the way he seemed to kiss the words as he spoke them, how his hands drifted together as if he were praying while his gaze slipped toward the window, and how his voice, that voice so low and smoky, seemed to rattle the metal fittings on those old fixed desks, a bass line that sank the class deep into their seats. He made me see, which is my life's blood now, by watching him. What I saw, and this was physical alone, was style, grace, authority, and an aspect of vision. I wanted to know his story and, perhaps, be part of it.

I say this now, of course, because as a student of literature I was a pretty sorry specimen. In Dr. Cassell's American survey course I remember tying myself up in knots trying to interpret the symbolism of the insect in Dickinson's poem "I heard a fly Buzz when I died." When I mentioned this to his colleague Dr. Baetzhold recently, he said, "Thought it was the soul or something?" Yes, yes, how did he know? It was that obvious. Dr. Cassell, I remember, talked me back to earth. He walked out from behind his desk toward me and stood by the window. As I sputtered on, he stared out through the leaded glass, asked a question that fogged the pane. What was it he said then? I can't remember. It doesn't matter what the poem means. Now I only remember the posture of the man, the light in the window, that soothing voice, the deep harmonic of its own buzz.

I also weaseled my way into an independent study with him. Ford Madox Ford. I ascribed to the theory that things would rub off if I just got nearby. But my performance was truly awful. I froze, couldn't write a thing because by that time I idealized Professor Cassell so much that nothing I wrote would be good enough. A terrible fate to befall a professor. A student hanging on every word, a goofy kid trying to impress instead of learn something.

Right! I pretended to do research in the library and was driven slowly mad by the drippy little fountain in the atrium. I'd hide in the stacks when Professor Cassell marched through, angling toward the rare book room to teach his graduate class. I'd watch him handle the books, watch him make notes. There was not much doing on the campus then, and I'd hate to think that a student of mine stalks me now the way I stalked him. But then, we always live in the age of lead, and my obsession had to do with the precious metal I assayed in the man. I had tinkered with his character in my imagination. I was screwed up for sure. It is not that I want to say that he was so great a teacher—he was a great teacher—but that back then he bore my schoolboy adoration with such finesse and care. He was finally himself, and that was truly fine.

I got a B in the independent study. I remember he wrote me a letter. I had transferred to IU by then. It said to write, write, write, learn how to spell, write, and write some more.

I told Susan, as we drove by the shopping center where that used clothing store had been, that the conventional wisdom of buying secondhand holds that you want the clothes of someone who has recently died. The living only give away things when they are worn-out or outgrown. The best stuff comes from the dead. I walked around Butler's campus for three years in a dead man's coat, shadowing the man I wanted to become, a pale ghost. I tried to rig a life for myself from the scraps I found as I followed in his wake. What more can a student ask for? Now I do remember something from one of his classes, the short story course, where we read Gogol's "The Overcoat." I remember what Professor Cassell said Turgenev said about the story. "We all come from beneath 'The Overcoat.'" Indeed.

Bob Sullivan, my roommate, did pledge Teke. It was the age of streaking, and Bob was kicked out of school for a while when he was caught with a band of brothers streaking, strolling really, through the lobby of Switzer, the women's dorm, on parents' weekend. He was never really happy in the house and would come back over to the dorm every once in a while. He kept his phonograph records in my room, including some albums of Gregorian chants. One spring day, while the Sigma Chis were playing Iron Butterfly for the hundredth time for the neighborhood, I hoisted Bob's stereo speakers into my own windows and cranked up the Benedictine monks to compete against the heavy metal with its monotonic howling. Dr. Cassell was walking by on his way home. The angelic host weaved its Latin plosives between an electric guitar feedback, a solo lick. I saw Dr. Cassell stop, cock his head to listen, and look up toward my window. I saw him looking for the music. He would have loved the juxtaposition, the sacred and the profane. I love this memory most of all. This little squall on his daily voyage home that broke his stride. And that is always how I'll remember him: that stomping walk of his as he walked away to the beat of the music of the spheres. Can you see him? Can you see him turning now and walking once more for home?

After Words

A FOREWORD

Anna Leahy asked me to write this afterword for an anthology she was putting together called *The Authority Project* that collected papers on the pedagogy of creative writing. I wrote it last summer, the summer of 2004, beginning on Memorial Day while the war was going on in Iraq, at about the time of the first revelation of American torture in the prisons there and at the same time the massive World War II Memorial opened in Washington. As I was putting together this book, I got word from Anna that her publisher thought my contribution was problematic and requested "a more clearly organized piece that is more directly connected to the essays that precede it and that more directly addresses the issue of authority, which guides the book." So I present here, as an afterword to this book, this rejected afterword, a foreword for the words to follow, disorganized and indirect and with little or no authority on authority.

We are shut up in schools and college recitation rooms for ten or fifteen years, and come out at last with a bellyful of words and do not know a thing. We cannot use our hands, or our legs, or our eyes, or our arms. We do not know an edible root in the woods. We cannot tell our course by the stars, nor the hour of the day by the sun. It is well if we can swim or skate. We are afraid of a horse, of a cow, of a dog, of a cat, or a spider. Far better was the Roman rule to teach a boy nothing he could not learn standing.
RALPH WALDO EMERSON

As I write this, thousands are gathering in Washington, D.C., to dedicate the new memorial. It has been some sixty years in the making. Chronologically, the war it commemorates precedes the wars in Korea and Vietnam, but both of those later conflicts have their own well-established and venerated shrines nearby. Part of what slowed construction of the World War II Memorial had to do with where to place it. Its contested site, the one being opened today between the Washington Monument and the Lincoln Memorial, drastically reconfigures the historic Mall. Symbolically (and that is what it is all about here) the World War II Memorial is to be seen, finally, as the seminal event of America's American Century, the twentieth one, sandwiched between the marble cenotaphs of the country's two previous centuries.

The continuous media coverage of the event has been structured around a litany of numbers. There were 16 million Americans in uniform in World War II, we are reminded. We are shown the 4,000 stars affixed to one curving wall of the memorial, each star representing 100 who died, some 400,000 in all. But the one number that the announcers and commentators keep coming back to gains real heft, embedded as it is in the narrative of mortality and time and the long delay of this recognition. It is the number that makes this monument imperative, a mortal clock. 1,000. One thousand, we are told. One thousand veterans of the war die each day. The survivors of the 16 million now number fewer than 3 million, and 1,000 die each day. Memorials are always actuarial tables in stone. This one, perhaps, even more than most, consciously sculpts the figures.

Of course this monument had to be cut in solid stone, the preferred material for the illusion of time immemorial, but if I were to design my own tribute, I think I would put up, overnight, a grid of corrugated metal Quonset huts. You know, those prefabricated half-pipes of steel (the wall becoming roof becoming wall) scalloped together, one after the other. My Quonset hut village would recall for the vet the ubiquitous look and feel of camp or base. The veterans would remember the hurried construction, thrown up overnight, a domestication of the chaos, an elegant stay against confusion. These buildings speak to both the ingenuity unleashed in war and the faceless industrial nature of its modern manifestation. The Quonset hut prefigured Levittown, the collective dream so many returning troops fell into, but the hut also reminds us all that the buildings themselves were habitats after the war. Quonset huts were the "temporary" housing on countless college campuses, bivouacking countless GIs cashing in the benefits offered in the GI Bill. I've worked at five different universities, and all five of them maintained their nests of Quonsets. Visiting other campuses, one still sees the scattering of buildings, these new ruins of time and space. Occasionally an administration would launch a campaign suggesting that the "temporary" housing's time had come only to be met with howls of protest from nostalgic alumni who matriculated in those steel shells, and there, in their newly married state, generated a good part of my generation in one big and famous boom.

I propose the Quonset hut, then, as symbol of something more permanent than temporary. It is a symbol too of that legislation. The law is the true legacy. The way I see it that little piece of paper, the GI Bill, is the reason why I teach writing, why so many of us teach writing, on a college campus still, landscaped by the remaining rings of barracks, the permanent "temporary."

Those GIs were kids, mostly. Most of them fought the war out of high school. The war consumed their college years. Paul Fussell's most recent book on the subject is called *The Boys' Crusade*. And Kurt Vonnegut's *Slaughterhouse-Five* is also known as *The Children's Crusade*. Remember, there were 16 million of them, and all of these children, if they wanted, could go to college as they were demobed. And in those millions there had to be a battalion or two made up of soldiers who wanted to write fiction and poetry. And with cash in hand they showed up to occupy the few classrooms dedicated to the teaching of fiction and poetry writing—Iowa, Hopkins, Syracuse. . . .

Two generations after this initial invasion of world war veterans, I occupied the same seats and the same classrooms, and in two generations since have taught there too. Much has changed, but we are talking about the notion of authority and its presence in the creative writing classroom. I wanted here to invoke some essential ingredients of the creative writing classroom's initial claim to authority.

I always find it curious—the residue that survives time. I currently teach at a university, Alabama, where all of its classroom buildings are built in a neoclassical style, Greek temples with pillars and pediments. What makes these classical buildings look authentically, well, classic are the accoutrements of the detailing. There above the pillars, for example, are the triglyphs, squares of stone etched with three parallel vertical vestigial indentations, a characteristic of the ancient style. But what do they represent? No one knew, until recent archaeology suggested that their origins could be found in their wooden predecessors. The triglyphs are lithic representations of the end caps of wooden roof support beams of the original temples. In those later Hellenistic times when wood gave way to stone, the masons recreated the wood in the new media. You already were changing the material of the houses of the gods; you didn't want to mess too much with the formula of expression. You make the stone look like wood. It is always the case that what we've done in the past becomes obscure, forgotten. It is also the case that we replicate in the present those long-ago codified gestures, habits, rituals. Centuries later we are still carving triglyphs to cap the columns of the buildings because it has always been thus. The primal utility has gone out of the gesture, but the gesture itself has not vanished. It is all aesthetic now but no less powerful. It still looks like a temple.

When it comes to the authority of the creative writing classroom, I think it is important to consider what rooms we currently inhabit and what we have inherited from the initial conception, what triglyph-like residue we replicate.

We shouldn't forget, then, that workshops and creative writing programs were started and promulgated by punk kids who had just won a world war. One such kid, James B. Hall, a veteran of the European theater, was in the initial postwar class at Iowa and went on to found the writing program at Oregon and then establish the new experimental college at Santa Cruz. Many of these founders were field grade officers like Hall, but just as many were enlisted soldiers or marines. They brought to those early classrooms already rich and complex ideas about authority and hierarchies as well as an abundance of practical experiential knowledge.

Remember this is the generation of writers, a generation we now routinely call the greatest, that created the words to condense one aspect of their recent history into understated acronymic shorthand. *Snafu* and *fubar* stood for all the catch-22s in which they found themselves caught up. The Kafka-esque bureaucracies, the creepy chains of commands. "Chickenshit," Paul Fussell calls it in an essay on the subject, delineating such trivialities as military courtesy and the fussy triplication of every piece of paper in sight. At the same time, these same soldiers were fighting a real war not simply bureaucratic battles. In spite of the petty sniping from the rear, life and death problems were being confronted and mastered in the front, often through highly imaginative and elegant methods. The stalled breakout at Normandy comes to mind, with armies of tanks bogged down in the impenetrable hedgerows of France. The improvisational initiative of some sergeant in the ranks who had the idea to weld a rack of hedge-cutting steel teeth on a tank did the trick.

What I am attempting to recreate here in brief is the unique set of circumstances present at the creation of this discipline. Present was a democratic enlisted personnel entrepreneurial gung-ho-ness combined with the same personnel's residual trauma derived from the recently transpired events that resulted in a profound inarticulateness and alienation from the naive home front. Present also was a deep and abiding suspicion of all authority even as the lessons of power had been deeply absorbed and naturalized. Ingrained in these new students was the preference for knowledges derived from actual experience, hands-on physical experience over smarts that trumped mere book learning. The academy, then, would not be their natural habitat.

And there is the great irony, that these khaki-clad students, prepared by life, should find themselves, sixty years ago, leaving one theater of operations for another. I try to remind myself how strange that must have been for them, that first wave of poets and fiction writers taking up stations on the fields of academe. Years later, I believe we all suspect that we suffer the fallout from this great migration, that we labor still under their influence in the ruins of what they built up out of ruins they inherited and helped also to create.

Of all the gin-joints in all the world. The coincidences of history are stunning and certainly dramatic. These government-issued creative writers, already biased with an abiding ambiguity toward authority and a history of hard-knocks experience they learned, as it were, standing, now fell into this new state of affairs. They would make the best of it at the university, a medieval institution founded on the idea that knowledge was fiduciary, held in trust by experts who initiated the acolyte to the secrets of such things as medicine, law, theology.

Not that the university itself had been immune from mutating influences once the institution was established here and forced to open its doors and classrooms to the subject matter of the masses. Its mission was already deflected in crazy ways. I taught at Iowa State University, a land-grant institution. Many of my students were from farms and were studying, they believed, to return there. I asked them one day if they thought I could take and pass their classes in agronomy, genetics, animal husbandry, and the like. Sure, they answered.

"And," I said, "I would be a farmer, right?"

"Well, no," they replied, adding that one would have to grow up on the farm as they had. So I asked the obvious question.

"Why are you here then studying to be a farmer?"

Part of the answer was for the credential, the license that the institution in its fiduciary mode loves to endow. Another truth was that studying farming was not going to return them to the farm to be better farmers, the idealism of another government act—the land-grant one. No, a farming degree put wheels on your feet, propelled you off the farm and into the larger concerns of business, agribusiness or otherwise, where one could farm the abstract knowledge one had mastered at school. Funny that this conversation played out in a course I taught on contemporary rural and agricultural literature — the recent writing of Wendell Berry, Richard Rhodes, Mary Swander, Jane Smiley. My students did not recognize the subject matter as important.

"What should we be studying?" I asked.

"Something important, you know. Like the Greek and Roman classics."

The class always turned existential. Even though it started with the farm content, the class always led back to issues of education and knowledge. It was always about itself and focused on what is taught, should be taught, where and how someone learns and for what purpose.

So American college classrooms are fraught, always it seems, by this anxiety, this drama enacted by the opposing ideas of the nature of knowledge and our conflicted, complicated ideas of authority.

As I write this, I am mulling over other issues of knowledge and authority that seem legion in this season. The cicadas sing. On the day Venus transits the sun, my black-eyed Susans open. Other things transpire. Details of the tortures inflicted by American soldiers upon prisoners in Iraq accumulate, and with those details the famous postwar studies of coercion and power are dusted off. About the time the above-remembered GIs were entering universities here at home, a university study demonstrated that most of us would participate in and perpetrate torture and even murder if the conditions were right. And the right conditions needed only to be, it seemed, a white-coated, articulate man uttering a few well-chosen, liberating words.

"You have no choice," he says when the subjects of the experiment begin to protest what they have been asked to do. "You must go on. I take full responsibility." And that seemed to be enough. It is enough for most of us to electrocute someone, to pull the trigger, to torture. I heard one sociologist comment on television that this is not so much a question of bad apples. We should all understand that any apple could be made bad given the right conditions. Authority is appealing when appealed to.

After Memorial Day, D Day was commemorated as well. The dwindling number of eyewitnesses, the authenticators of the experience, spoke the powerful words and formulas to remember. And bizarrely too the last known Confederate widow died that same week as I typed these words. She was the last physical link to another war, another war that now can only be reenacted, the evidence of its event, reduced mainly to mere words, endlessly sifted through. There were eulogies and speeches. And, oh yes, a former president who lived a decade or more not remembering a thing was remembered in death and was buried, surrounded by the trappings of great and sustained power. And just today another former president, a living one, unveiled his official portrait whose newsworthy sidebar was that the image was rendered by an artist characterized as self-taught, as unschooled, as an outsider.

It is not only teachers of this particular art, the wranglers of words, who wrestle with the mantles of authority, earned or inherited. The whole culture grapples with who is in charge and what can be known, who must be listened to and what must be remembered. As authors, authors sense acutely the complicated relationship they have with authority. "Author" and "authority" — it goes beyond the mere suffix following the word. In the classroom or out of it, what one speaks, what one writes is always seeking a purchase, looking for traction, hoping this word will take.

How strange is that current Xerox commercial being broadcast on television? It advertises the newish technology of on-demand publishing. The setting is a creative writing classroom, but creative writing teachers know it is like no creative writing classroom they know. The teacher (is he in a turtleneck, a corduroy blazer?) stands imperiously at the front of a large lecture hall, lecturing on the impossibility of publishing, reeking with authority. He intones with great command presence. Listen: there is this hint of what

English dialect? It is English English, I think. It is impossible to get published, he booms. And one might expect that the quality of the work, whatever that is (and that is the rub for us, isn't it, whether we are teaching or studenting?), would be the winnowing factor in the scarcity of publishing opportunities. But no. It is "the expense," the cost, that is at issue. And at that moment a dumpy, stuttering student clumsily interjects, takes issue with the issue and, gaining strength and clarity, pimps the new printing process. Score one for the little guy. Everyone knows how to write. What is not known is the technology of publishing. All the other students cheer, make plans to self-publish. They demand on-demand. The teacher deflates within his chalk-smudged jacket. The writing and the teaching of writing are so beside the point. We like to believe that to be an author is to author a book, but it may be enough simply to make a book, the object itself, in order to be an "author."

And as I revise and proof these pages, these words, reports cross my desk that I must now post as amendments to the above. A new Confederate widow has emerged and the "unschooled" official presidential portrait artist turns out to have a BFA and MFA from Temple. So much for my authority of facts, my knowledge of what is what.

And this just in. The Supreme Court has today thrown out the case involving the removal of two words — "under God" — from the Pledge of Allegiance. A technicality. The father who brought the suit in the name of his daughter had no custodial standing. The court acts on this technicality and avoids the issue of the establishment of religion in the classroom. For now, "God" is back in.